Bad Love

Identifying and Getting Out of a Bad Relationship

Dr. Mary Ann Martínez

MARCASA BOOKS

Marcasa Books
PO Box 5442
Caguas, PR 00726

This book contains information that is intended to help the readers be better informed. It is presented as general advice and do not intend to diagnose any health and/or mental health illness. Always consult your doctor or psychotherapist for your individual needs. This book is not intended to be a substitute for the professional advice of a licensed therapist or licensed physician. The reader should consult with their healthcare professional in any matters relating to his/her mental health.

Dedication

To everyone that finds themselves struggling with feelings and decisions, still believing in love and second chances... remember that every end is, in fact, a new beginning.

Contents

"A bad relationship is like standing on broken glass, if you stay you will keep hurting. If you walk away, you will hurt, but eventually you will heal."

-- Autumn Kohler

Introduction

We all go into relationships for happiness – to find that one person we are destined to live with forever and ever. Love is indeed a beautiful feeling and being in a relationship with someone special could give us more joy than anything else in this world. When we enter a relationship with someone we like, we are always full of positivity, enthusiasm, and hope. We envision sharing a lifetime with each other; although there are ups and downs in every relationship, the general goal is to stay happy together.

But unfortunately, that is not how most of these relationships end. While there might be some lucky couple who get to grow old with each other, others drift apart – if not actually separate from each other but grow weary of their life together.

I am a psychotherapist and I have worked with couples in distress for the last 25 years. I have seen couples come in for help because they are absolutely confused of where their relationship had gone wrong, what they were missing from their life together and why they were growing drained of each other. Most of all, they were just unhappy with the way life was going! Among most of the couples I have helped, it was almost impossible for them to tell me why they were unhappy or what made them discontent, just that they were feeling dissatisfied with their lives, and most importantly, with each other.

I am not talking about relationships where one or both partners had been unfaithful, or when they are abusive and mean. These couples had the perfect relationships, at least on the outside. Their reasons for unhappiness were not always easy to understand. On the surface, they had everything someone would want in a relationship. I have seen couples who look perfectly happy with each other but in truth, are feeling trapped inside. What's worse is that they themselves can't explain why they are feeling this way, but only that they are not happy with their partners.

They say 1 in every 3 marriages end in divorce; understandingly, the number of breakups everywhere is alarmingly higher than divorce rates. According to the Business Insider[1], European countries have the highest number of divorces, much more than anywhere else in the world. In Belgium, 7 out of 10 marriages end in divorce, whereas the numbers are around 53% in the United States. When the official rates are so astonishingly high all around the world, it is really surprising that most of the relationships around us fail and end in tears?

---

[1] https://www.businessinsider.com/map-divorce-rates-around-the-world-2014-5

Not every relationship in distress can be salvaged. Some people are just trapped in a bad relationship even when their partners are not abusing them in any way, or being violent, or unfaithful, or even disrespectful or inattentive. But before you can decide which way to go, you need to determine if you really are in a bad relationship or not, and why. You need to observe yourself, your partner, and your relationship under a microscope to know just where you went wrong, and what to do about it.

This book, **"Bad Love:** *Identifying and Getting Out of a Bad Relationship"*, will help you in this journey. It is for everyone – for people who are going through a rough phase in their relationship, as well as for people who are thinking of getting out. My goal with this book is that you will hopefully be able to understand where your relationship went wrong, and whether it is possible for you to recover from the rut you are in. Moreover, if you really want out of your 'Bad Love', better do it the right way than to make a mess of things – all of which you can find described in this book.

Besides, if you are a Marriage and Family Therapist like me, this book can hopefully work as a guideline to understand everything that a person goes through when they are in a not-so-obvious bad love and/or contemplating ending their relationship. I have used 25 years' worth of experience in this field to write this book, and I will consider it my great honor if others in my profession are benefitted from my efforts.

This book can be the perfect guideline for you when you are feeling dissatisfied with your relationship and want a way out, or when you are looking for answers of why you don't feel the happiness in your commitments that you used to feel before. So, if you are in the place where thousands of couples all around the world find themselves at some point in their life, I hope this book helps you to some extent.

Wish you all the best!

Section I: Are You in a Bad Relationship?

All around the world, men and women in committed relationships asks themselves this question at least once in their lifetimes: *Am I happy in this relationship?*

This is not something uncommon in relationships – whether you have been married to each other for 10 years or in a six-month old relationship with someone. It is normal to doubt our happiness level when we are committed to another person, and this question can come after a simple argument or after years of discontent. However, when things are really going downhill for you both, this is a question that is going to haunt you almost every moment, every day of your life. Feeling angry or dissatisfied after an argument is fine, but not when you are feeling this all the time. That is when you should understand this: *there must be something actually wrong with your relationship!*

Relationships are not simple; it takes a lot for two people to stay committed to each other and stay happy together. Intimacy, physical attraction, friendship, laughter, understanding – these are all part of a successful relationship. The absence of one or more of these will make you feel like something vital is missing from your life, and it's not your fault if that is how you are feeling. When you have committed to another person and living together, you need something more than just feelings for that person.

It is true that love for that special someone makes us want to commit to them, but only love is not enough to live together happily ever after. As a matter of fact, you need three different elements, as described by the renowned psychiatrist Robert J. Sternberg in his "Triangular Theory of Love" presented in 1985.

Sternberg's Triangular Theory of Love

Robert J. Sternberg was a member of the Yale University Psychology Department, and a professor of the same faculty. He worked extensively with human interpersonal relationships, especially in the fields of wisdom, intelligence, creativity, ethical reasoning, hate and love. One of his most important presentations was the "Triangular Theory of Love" which he first talked about in 1985.

According to this theory[2], there are three main components of love – passion, intimacy, and decision/commitment. Without even one of this, even the deepest of love between two people cannot be complete.

Passion refers to the physical attraction between a couple, one that is related to romance and sexual consummation. This is only possible in a romantic relationship where two people need to be sexually

---

[2] http://www.robertjsternberg.com/love

attracted to each other. Evidently the intensity of sexual behavior in a couple changes over time, but in a happy couple, some form of passionate love is always present.

Other than just the physical attraction, passion can also be referred to the strong desire, enthusiasm or feeling of excitement that both partners feel in a relationship – a feeling that is not just sexual. This could be the strong passion to protect each other, the immense jealousy that partners often feel in some situation, or the desire to keep each other safe from harm. Needless to say, this is part of staying happy with a single partner; if either or both partners feel the lack of passions – either sexual or any other type – in their relationship, it becomes very tough to continue that relationship.

Intimacy is also especially important in relationships and refers to the close bonding a couple feels among themselves. In a marriage or a committed relationship, it is the feeling of "us against the whole world" that makes a couple feel intimate with each other. Inside jokes, enjoying time with each other, laughing together, intimate non-sexual touches – these are what bring two people close. People who are intimate are completely at ease with each other and this, according to Sternberg, is a crucial part of a relationship.

Decision/Commitment is the conscious decision that one or both partners take to stay together.

A marriage is the ultimate commitment a couple takes to stay with each other in the long term; having children together, moving in together, living together, or being an exclusive couple are other commitments that couples take. It is not enough for a couple to just be passionate about each other or to be intimate when they do not make the conscious decision to stay together. It is the commitment and the decision between a couple that can prove just how strong their attachment to each other is. Without the commitment to exclusively stay together, a couple cannot be happy with each other.

In the "Triangular Theory of Love", all three of these emotions are imagined to be the three angles of a triangle. In a perfect relationship, all three emotions – intimacy, passion, and commitment/decision – interact with each other. A great passion between both partners lead to ease and intimacy between them, which encourages them to be committed to each other; in the same way, in a committed relationship, passion for each other is inevitable.

If one emotion is less than the others in a relationship, it is the other emotions that strengthen the relationship. For example, in a relationship where the couple had been married for many years, the physical passion may decrease a little, but the level of intimacy increases manifold over time, as does the commitment to stay with each other.

The absence of any one of these three emotions can change the love between couples; there are eight types of "limiting" love that can occur between two people, as distinguished by Sternberg himself. In "infatuated Love", only passion is present but not intimacy or commitment; in "Romantic Love", it is commitment that is absent, but passion and intimacy is in abundance. In an "Empty Love", which can be the case of an arranged marriage, only commitment is present without any passion or intimacy. It is only in true and consummated love that all three emotions are present in almost equal amounts.

Robert J. Sternberg's "Triangular Theory of Love" is still today one of the simplest yet complete definitions of love to live by. Through these three important components, as described in this theory, can a couple be truly fulfilled with each other in a relationship. The absence of even one of them completely changes the love felt between them and makes them unhappy with each other.

Sternberg is, at present, a Professor of Cornell University in the College of Human Ecology, as well as an Honorary Professor at Heidelberg University in Germany. He lives in Ithaca, New York with his wife and five children.[3]

---

[3] http://www.robertjsternberg.com

Looking into Your Own Relationship

To answer the age-old question of whether you are happy in your relationship, you need to apply Sternberg's theory in your life, which is not always easy. When you have been with someone for many years, it is not possible to suddenly measure the level of intimacy, passion and commitment you have for each other.

What you can do is ask yourselves a few questions, and the answers will help you realize where your relationship is suffering, or where it has gone wrong so that you are unhappy with your partner of choice. Just answer these following questions truthfully, to identify the possible reasons.

How did your Relationship Start?

Yes, the very start of your relationship is particularly important to determine its future.

If you are in your late 30s and have been together since high school, it is definite that you are very much compatible with each other to last for so many years. High school sweethearts will often *tena* to have happy, less conflict-laden marriages, even if they eventually end up divorced for some reason.[4] In part, this is because

---

[4] https://brandongaille.com/20-high-school-sweethearts-marriage-statistics

they share an intimacy and a friendship that is rare in other couples. These kinds of couples grow up together and are more at ease with each other because after the long courtship, they know almost everything there is to know.

On the other hand, some marriages are of convenience, i.e., when two people who have not been courting for long decides to get married either because they are expecting a child together or because of family pressures. These marriages have a lower chance of lasting because marriage may not have been the desired end of their courtship. It is entirely possible that a couple dating each other didn't even want to be together, maybe because they are not in love or feel they don't know each other enough, but was pressured into marrying because of an unintentional pregnancy or other "convenience".

On the other hand, even though there is research[5] finding that rebound romances have some benefits, these types of relationship also almost never last. When someone is recently heartbroken or just out of a long romance, it is common for them to get involved with another person too soon. But a rebound relationship can merely be a distraction so that the heartbroken person does not think about their ex. In this kind of

---

[5] Brumbaugh, C. C. & Fraley, R.C. (2015) Too fast, too soon? An empirical investigation into rebound relationships. *Journal of Social and Personal Relationships,* 32(1), 99-118.

relationships, the new man/woman is just someone to spend time with and be intimate with so that the pain of the recent heartbreak can be tolerated. In other words, the person on rebound is using the new relationship until they get over the old one, and once they are past the initial pain of their old breakup, they might not need that new person in their life anymore.

In many cases, both parties are on rebound with each other; both partners are using the same relationship to get over their previous heartbreaks. These relationships often never last for more than a few weeks, or months, and are more about physical attraction than anything else. If they do get serious, they eventually drift apart after the initial attraction fades away. Sometimes, it is within a few months; at other times, they may even last a few years together.

Some relationships start based on wanting the wrong things in life. Marrying someone for wealth or family name or being attracted to a person just because of their outer beauty, getting involved with someone famous, marrying into a business or a political family – these are some of the wrong reasons that two people get involved. In these cases, the external factors are more important than the actual people getting involved in the relationship and is bound to result in dissatisfaction within a short time.

Many relationships out there start because the two people involved are physically attracted to each other. It's not the personality or the character of the other person that attracts them, or even their traits and thoughts, but just their physical compatibility. These relationships are born out of lust, rather than love. Intimacy is present to some extent in these relationships, but they are doomed to end early before real commitment makes an appearance.

Also condemned are the relationships that start while one or both partners are still committed to someone else. Affairs that break up marriage and destroy families may be full of passion, but also riddled with guilt and ill-wish. In most of the cases, when two people cheat on their own commitments to be with someone else, the new relationship – however passionate or intimate – sooner or later fades away into nothing. Very few people, after cheating on their spouses or partners, can live happily with each other in their new relationship.

How your relationship started is, to a great extent, responsible for how fast it decays, or how unhappy you feel in it. When you are feeling dissatisfied with your love life, try and remember how it started because it can give us an idea of the depth and quality of your relationship.

If you had started your relationship in a normal fashion – i.e., the natural course of meeting someone you like, getting to know them gradually and then committing to each other – chances are, it is not your beginning that is the problem. A slow and steady start of a life together gives you the time to decide for yourself whether you want to spend your life with that particular person. If something goes wrong later, there are other factors to blame rather than how your relationship started.

As I said, there are relationships which start for the wrong reasons – getting married because you are going to have a child, choosing someone because of their looks, wealth, title, or social standing, arranged marriages, being forced into marriages for the sake of society, getting involved with someone on the rebound, or simply out of loneliness, etc. In all of these situations, there is one thing is common: *something is forcing these people to make a commitment to each other.* The people they end up with are not someone who was their first choice, or even a conscious choice. Is it such a wonder that relationships that start for the wrong reasons often fail to last?

Of course, there are exceptions to this! There are thousands of examples of marriages that started for the wrong reasons, where both partners end up being very happy with each other or strangers who get involved on a rebound end up happily ever after. Star-crossed lovers find each other when they are in their late 40s, married to someone else. When it comes to relationships and love, there is no strict rule to follow. Just because your beginning was bumpy, it does not mean your ending is near. Still, it can be quite the opposite in your case!

This is more of a general rule that does not necessarily have to apply to everyone. But as a generalization, relationships that do not start and grow in a natural developmental way are more likely to fail than relationships that start in an uncomplicated situation. Either ways, the start is always important; it's the beginning that gives us an idea of your life together in the future.

Are You Friends?

More than in any other relationships, friendship is important between couples.

Remember Monica and Chandler from F.R.I.E.N.D.S.? One of the most important reasons they made such an amazing onscreen couple is because they were friends first and then a couple. As friends, they knew each other's faults and shortcomings better than anyone else. That is what made them a powerful couple, because friendship makes a relationship more concrete than just physical compatibility.

Relationships are much more than lovey-dovey nicknames for each other and red roses on Valentine's Day. A relationship cannot just survive on passion and commitment if you are not friends with each other; you need friendship to have that special intimacy between yourselves.

Whether a couple were friends before their relationship or not, it is definitely important for them to be friends later when they are officially a couple. Friendship is the ideal complement to romance – it gives you the chance to laugh together, to have fun together, and to enjoy yourselves doing simple things. In an ideal world, your partner should be a best friend with whom you are planning to spend your whole life together. While you should have other best friends, your partner should definitely be one of the people you are closest to in this world. This does not mean that they are people you are physically close to and enjoy intimacy with, but someone you can talk to and share your thoughts with.

It is actually hard not to be friends with someone you live with and spend so much time with. If you are not friends, it means that you are not your true self in front of your significant other. Either you are maintaining a formal facade – which is common in the early days of a new relationship; or you are deceiving both of you by being someone completely different than the person that you are.

But what happens when you are friends first, and lovers/partners second? You can be yourself and not worry about your significant one not liking you for it. You can show your true inner self to your partner and not scare them off with your uniqueness; you won't have to hide your true feelings, ideas and thoughts because you are afraid they'd be misunderstood. Friendship lets you be you in a relationship and makes you ready for everything that can happen to you.

So, how do you know you are friends? There are no definite rules, but there are some telltale signs of couples who are also friends.

— You will be able to share everything together – all your ideas, dreams and thoughts, no matter how ridiculous or far-fetched.

— You can talk about your dreams and aspirations without facing judgment from your partner.

— You can talk about your letdowns without feeling like a failure.

— You can always find something fun to do together.

— You can be honest with each other, even when you have done something wrong.

—   You have inside jokes and stories that no one else has access to.

—   Your memories are of fun incidents, not just romantic ones.

—   You can disagree or fight and make-up instantly, without any damages done.

—   You can say anything to each other, even intimate topics you can only discuss with a best friend; and many more.

Most importantly, being friends gives you the ease and intimacy that only comes with knowing a person for many, many years. Just as much romance and passion is important in a relationship, friendship is more important. If you are a couple who are not friends, first and foremost, this could be a reason behind all the problems in your relationship.

It is very important that you are friends with the person you have decided to spend your life with, no matter how you met or started out in the beginning. Without friendship, your relationship is bound to become formal and boring, and that is no way to live your life as a couple.

Are You Compatible?

Relationships are where two very different people come together, but still find ways to be compatible with each other. However, sometimes two people are so different from each other, it may be hard for them to adjust.

"Opposites Attract", yes! But there is a limit to how compatible two people can be together when they are completely different from each other. Take for example a couple where one partner is a complete workaholic and immensely ambitious, and the other one is someone who can't hold on to a simple job for more than a week. Think about it, are these two people really compatible together?

We all love the 1990 movie "Pretty Woman" (with actress Julia Roberts and actor Richard Gere), but is that scenario really possible in real life? Can two people so completely different from each other live together when the initial fascination is over? Fairy tale endings are lovely, but when reality knocks at the door, is it really happily ever after for everyone? Perhaps you think I am being a little too negative, but as a couple's therapist, I have found it important for two people in a relationship to be compatible with each other, in as many ways as possible – physically, emotionally, sexually, socially, politically, and religiously!

It doesn't matter if you like pizza when your partner likes sushi; what matter is that you are compatible on a more basic level and agree on topics that are important to your life together. As a couple you have to make a number of decisions together that are going to affect your lives forever. If you differ too much in your opinions regarding these matters, it may be a problem later.

Sex and physical intimacy is very important in relationships, more for some couples than others. Although physical attraction and sexual behavior can change a little as the years roll over, it is an important part of a healthy relationship. At the start of a relationship, physical attraction plays a vital role which gives way to intimacy and love. If two people are not compatible physically, it is unlikely their relationship would advance very far, despite the amount of love and respect they have for each other.

How can a couple be physically mismatched? When one partner is sexually adventurous and interested in experimenting while the other partner adverse to it – that is one way the couple is going to get frustrated very soon! For some people, the physical part of a relationship is very important, and for a few others – an unpleasant task they have to endure. If these two people come together as a couple, the odds of their relationship surviving are slim.

Although not so much these days, religion also plays an important role in relationships. This is especially a problem if both partners are from different religions and have been brought up under strict religious scruples. A number of questions arise for them: how to celebrate the holidays, where and how to get married, whether or not to use birth control, what to name the children and how to raise them, whether to convert or not, and many others. When these questions arise for couples with different religious beliefs, they may become a problem if not treaded carefully and solved with care.

No matter how different you are from each other, it is always important that your basic ideals are the same, especially when it comes to decisions that are going to affect you both. For example:

—   When one partner wants children, and another is completely against having any.

—   When one partner (usually the male partner is most cases) don't want their partner (the woman, in these cases) to work after marriage.

—   When one partner object to another's choice of career, friends, hobbies, and other things.

–   When one partner (usually the male partner or the partner that brings more money into the household) wants to be the dominant one in the relationship who makes all the decisions at home.

These are aspects of your life where both partners need to be compatible with each other down to the last detail. Otherwise, one partner would become the victim, and ultimately unhappy, if you cannot mutually decide on these phases on your life together.

So, how can you understand if you are compatible with your partner/significant other? While every couple is different from another one, there are some common traits of a compatible couple, i.e.

–   When you understand each other's thought process and decision-making rituals without having to talk about them.

–   When you have the same core values in life.

–   When you come from similar, if not same, backgrounds with the same basic teachings from your families.

–   When you get on well with each other's family members.

— When you are compatible, if not close, to each other's friends.

— When you have a common friend circle to spend time with, together.

— When you are comfortable with the way your partner conducts themselves in front of company.

— When you have adequate respect about each other's career choice and work ethics.

— When you have a few similar interests together which you can enjoy with each other.

— When you are not afraid to fight or disagree with each other.

— When compromising for your partner comes easy for you in some matters.

— When you have differences, but which are acceptable to you both.

– When you are comfortable to spend time together doing your own personal chores.

– When you are physically attracted to each other even after years together.

– When you want to share all your good and bad news with your partner first and before anyone else; and many more.

True compatibility can come with knowing someone intimately and caring about them a lot, from the bottom of your heart. If your partner is someone you envision growing old together, compatibility can be worked together no matter how different you both are from each other. Compatibility between two partners in a relationship is the glue that holds it together. Nevertheless, there are some cases where compatibility cannot be achieved. Sometimes the differences are so profound that the couple is unable to adjust; specially if the adjustment represents something nonnegotiable for one of the partners.

When you are not compatible with each other – and when you do not or cannot make an effort to be so – your relationship could be in more trouble than you can salvage it from.

Can you be yourself in your Relationship?

It is extremely easy to forget ourselves in a relationship. Especially in the initial first few days or weeks, everything becomes about the new person we are with. There is hardly any time for individuality as we try to discover everything there is to know about the new and interesting person we are involved with.

Besides, in the initial days, we all prefer to spend as much time as we can with each other. Only the activities that can be shared are focused on, rather than our individual choices and needs. While this is completely normal in the beginning of a relationship, this should not be the case always. If you are in a relationship where you are slowly losing your individuality, it will not be possible for you to be happy in it.

Relationships should mean having fun with each other, but also keeping some space to breathe for yourself. A relationship where you are always spending time with your partner and only concentrating on your common interests can become very suffocating very quickly. It is especially important that you can be yourself – no judgments, no questions asked – when you are also a part of a relationship.

No matter how much you love your partner and how much you enjoy your time together, it is crucial that you give some time and effort to nourish the person you are, individually. It is never a good idea to let a relationship change you completely. Yes, the love of a true soul mate can make you a better person – someone more responsible, someone loving and caring, more organized, better balanced. But that does not mean you have to let go of the individual that you were before you got involved in this relationship. Otherwise, years down the lane, you will face an identity crisis, trying to remember the kind of person you were before you changed yourself for your partner.

A healthy relationship will definitely give you the breathing space to be yourself. It is important that you do not lose yourself too much in the initial romance that you can't find your own remains later.

Here are a few questions that you can ask yourself to understand whether you are being yourself in your relationship.

– Do you have friends of your own? Not mutual friends you hang out with as a couple, or your partner's friends you are close to, or family members you like spending time with. Friends who are yours only, perhaps from your life before you were in a relationship. School friends, college buddies, colleagues, ex-roommates, best friends – people who are your friends, and only remotely acquainted with your partner. To put it more exclusively: *these friends belong to you and you only, with whom you can talk about your life freely and at ease.*

– Do you spend time with your friends, without your partner? It could be just a cup of coffee, a drink after work or a weekend away with your friends, but it is particularly important that you spend time with your own friends, without your partner tagging along. There are always some topics that you need to talk about with your friends, and for these conversations, you need friends of your own. Sometimes it helps if your friends are the same sex as you, because you always need those "Ladies Night Out" or those "Sports Buddies" – generally speaking!

– Do you have hobbies and interests of your own, ones that your partner does not share? It is quite common if you do because it is almost impossible to find someone in this world who has your exact likes and dislikes. There must be something that you like doing that does not interest your partner, but that does not mean you have to completely abandon that hobby. Do not stop going to the movies just because your choice of films doesn't match; go with a friend or go alone because you want to. You can spend time together doing different things, as well. Just because your partner is watching the television does not mean you have to do the same; you can stay near and read, if that is what you like.

    – Do you always include your partner in your future plans? While that may be necessary in some cases, remember: *your partner does not have to be a part of everything you do!* You can make plans with your friends or family members without having to include the person you are in a relationship with. Whether it is a weekend getaway with your friends or a vacation with your parents – you can plan for your own. Even if you have the type of relationship where everything is consulted, still you should be able to plan activities without your partner, without that causing a crisis.

    – Do you constantly check up on your partner? It is not necessary, you know, to check up on each other throughout the day, or to let them know where you are and what you are doing. While keeping each other updated via texts or messages can be useful in some cases, it is absolutely unnecessary to make *obligatory* phone calls and messages throughout the day just to let them know you are thinking of them or to report on your activities.

Flirty texts, texts inquiring if they want something from the supermarket, texts to keep them updated about your children's whereabouts – these are all okay. Do you really need to send obligatory (emphasis on *obligatory*) "Thinking of you" or "I love you" texts just because you are used to them? Do you really need to know where they are and what they are doing all day? You really don't!

–   Do you feel obligated to experience every new thing with your partner? You do not have to, you know! If the movie you've been both eagerly waiting for finally hits the screen, you can make plans to watch it with your friends without feeling guilty about it. In the same way, your partner can plan a cross-country trip with their friends without you, and you should not be 'cross' about it.

–   Do you always speak as one unit? It is always "we like this" and "we hate that" with you? Although it may seem sweet to you, it can be annoying to others; chances are, your partner might not be a big fan of the "we" club either. Besides, when everything is a joint enterprise, you will be slowly losing your own identity in the relationship. So, if you have the habit of announcing everything as your joint venture, this is something you definitely need to stop.

– Do you let your partner speak for yourself? Even when it's something as simple as ordering for you or picking up your cell phone, this is not a healthy practice in a relationship. Just as everything should not be a "we" in your relationship, you should never be ashamed of speaking up for yourself. Never stop yourself from saying, "S/he loves it, but it's not for me."

– Do you talk about your relationship all the time, with everyone? There are thousands of topics to discuss about with your friends, family, and acquaintances, even your partner; only one of them should be about your relationship. You need to talk about a number of topics other than your partner, or where your relationship is going, or how happy you are, or how much you are enjoying yourself with your partner. Not everyone is going to enjoy listening about your romance all the time. You are under the risk of losing your own individuality when you go on and on about your relationship. Remember: *you are not your whole relationship; it is just a part of your life!*

It is of utmost importance that you don't lose yourself in your partner and in your relationship, no matter how deliriously happy you are. Never be afraid of being who you are, never stop standing up for yourself, and never let yourself go away because you are in a relationship.

How is the Environment at Home?

If the environment at home is tense, it is normal for you to feel suffocated in your relationship. On the other hand, a carefree and homely atmosphere can help your relationship flourish.

Whether you are married with children or a relatively new couple living together, your surrounding has a huge impact on your relationships. If you are two busy people who barely get the time to talk to each other during the day, always busy with your work, friends, and chores – is it a wonder when you feel alien in your own relationship? Compare your life to a couple who takes an effort to enjoy each other's company as much as they can, and you will see the difference in your lives.

Just because two people are living together under the same roof, it does not mean they are communicating well with each other. It could be that one or both are always too busy – with the children, with their jobs, with socializing, or the thousands of chores to complete around the house, to spend any time with each other. At the end of the day, you can be two strangers who live in the same room but barely talk to each other.

Is that something that has happened to your relationship? Does spending time together mean staring at the television, barely talking? Or disappearing into separate rooms after dinner to work on your career? Is all your time taken up by demanding children, visiting family members and friends dropping by? If these scenarios sound familiar to you, you are not the only one with this problem. There are thousands of relationships all around the world that are suffering because of a stifling environment at home.

The atmosphere at home should be one where both you and your partner can breathe easily. Your home should be a place where you want to go back to at the end of the day to spend time with your partner and family. If the condition back home is something that is driving you to spend more time at work or with your friends, it is not surprising if you want to get out of your relationship.

It happens to us all at one point in our life. We become so immersed in our children or our careers that we barely have time for our partners anymore. Our contact with each other becomes the bare minimum, where we can only talk in generalities. I have seen this happen to a lot of my clients over the years – the couple who used to stay awake all night talking to each other cannot barely sit down and share a meal together because they would have to communicate with each other. Instead of talking to each other about their feelings, they stare at the television together and call that 'family time'. Gradually, it becomes so stifling for them to spend some time together that they prefer to go out with their friends or work late.

If there is nothing that motivates you to go back home to your family at the end of the day, life can become unbearable to a person. Your relationship will seem oppressive because you will not be able to enjoy it anymore; never mind enjoy, your relationship will feel like a burden on your shoulders. So, take a good look at your family life and your home environment - is this what's happening to you?

– Do you feel terrible at the thought of going back home to your partner/family?

– Do you feel better when you are outside with your friends or at work, rather than at home?

– Do you always feel tensed and anxious at home?

– Do you have trouble communicating with your partner?

– Do you feel you have run out of topics to talk to your partner?

– Do you prefer to spend time alone at home instead of with your partner/family?

– Do you always watch what you say and do in front of your partner?

– Do you constantly feel criticized and judged by your partner?

– Do you entertain often at home because you don't want to be alone with your partner?

– Do you constantly make plans to go out or have people over so that you will not have to spend time alone with each other?

At the end of the day, does the thought of going home fill you with despair and dread – like you would rather be anywhere but at home? The environment at home may be responsible for you feeling like this. So, take a look at it when you have the time and decide: *is this the place where you want to spend the rest of your live?*

Have you Experienced Growth in your Relationship?

As we spend our days, weeks and months in a relationship, as human beings, we tend to grow with it. As our relationship grows, so do we, both because we grow in age and in experience. Love and intimacy make us grow up, so do responsibilities, commitment, and mutual understanding; sometimes, it is the true love of a soul mate that helps us to become the person we are.

The right relationship will never limit or stifle you; rather, people tend to grow more – personally, professionally, emotionally, and spiritually – when they encounter the right partner. How many men and women have succeeded to reach the pinnacle of their career because they have a supportive partner to encourage them? How many talented and creative people have given their best work after meeting their soul mate? Sometimes, it is our partners and loved ones who guide us to the right path and help us to excel.

There is an old proverb that was very famous for a long time: *behind every successful man, there is a woman.* Although this quote will not be very welcome in today's society, we can definitely agree on the fact that behind every successful man and woman, there is a loving partner who supports and helps them to succeed.

As I was saying, a healthy relationship will give you the chance to grow yourself rather than to limit your capabilities. I'm not only talking about your career, but your personal and emotional growth, as well as your spiritual advancement in life.

When a relationship first starts, the plans for the future are usually unrealistic, like a future seen through a pair of rose-colored glasses. Thousands of men and women all over the world begin their relationship promising that they:

• Will not become 'one of those' couples who fight with each other.

• Will not become 'one of those' couples who prefer to stay home every night instead of going out to party.

• Will not become 'one of those' couples who spend time watching television rather than talk to each other.

• Will not become 'one of those' couples who stop being sexually intimate with each other when they are older and weaker.

• Will not become 'one of those' couples who barely have time for each other because they've had children.

• Will not become 'one of those' couples who are more interested in their children's affairs than their own; and many more.

Real growth in a relationship comes when you

understand that these situations are something that happens to all of us at some point of our life, and that it is normal for our lives to change. A happy relationship does not refer to one where the couples are exactly where they started 10 years ago; rather, a successful relationship is where both partners have matured equally over time and accepted that their relationship with each other has matured with them.

Surely you cannot expect to be exactly in the same place with your partner when you are in your late 40s from where you first started together 20 years ago!

Growth is a regular process in a relationship. You can mature almost every day with the right partner by your side. Every time something happens in your life, you both grow a little more; it can be anything – your first major fight together, your first vacation, having a child together, getting a dog or a cat, buying a house, getting a promotion, losing a loved one, surviving an accident. Almost everything that happens to you – as a person and as a couple – helps you to develop and grow up.

It helps if your partner and you mature at the same level together; otherwise, it could be a problem if you are stuck at two different levels of maturity. If you are ready to settle down and have a child and your partner is still afraid of a commitment, it could definitely mean a problem for your life together.

How can you understand if you are having troubles in this regard in your relationship?

- When you have the feeling your partner does not understand your needs.
- When you feel your partner is disregarding your wishes for their own.
- When you feel your partner's plan for the future are very different from your own plans.
- When your partner's views and plans had not changed much over the years that you are together.
- When your partner seems immature and unable to take care of you and your family.
- When you cannot find anything to talk about with your partner.
- When you or your partner cannot accept the changes in your life over the years.
- When you cannot have a fight without getting serious about the situation, and many other such reasons.

Changes are inevitable in a relationship, and the best way to deal with them is to transform with these changes. Everything grows up around us – our children, our careers, our businesses, or our homes. But if we cannot keep up with these changes to grow as a couple, it will not be possible for us to survive in our relationships. Remember: *if you cannot grow up together, chances are, you have grown apart from each other, and that is not a healthy sign in a relationship!*

Are your Needs Satisfied?

Who is a soul mate? Someone who is the exact same person as you, someone who complements you absolutely? Someone whose thoughts, ideas and plans are completely identical to you? Someone who thinks like you and acts like you?

If you ask me, a soul mate is someone who is aware of your need and will not hesitate to make every effort to try and fulfill them. Being aware of your needs (or at least, trying to know what those needs are), especially if they are completely different from the ones of your partner – makes someone perfect with you. It does not matter if your partner is someone who is not similar to you in any way, or if their needs are different from yours; what makes them your perfect partner is if they have your best interest at heart.

Relationships, especially marriages, take a lot of work. We have a lot of expectations from our partners, and they need many commitments from us. What makes a relationship genuinely great is when a couple can anticipate and fulfill – or try their best to fulfill – each other's needs. After all, isn't that mainly why we enter into a relationship? When we find someone we can trust to do us good!

We have a lot of needs and demands in our life to be happy, and we mostly rely on our partner to participate in our own efforts to make them come true. This is the reason for choosing someone we find compatible to live with, because we are all looking for that special person who will make our dreams come true. Our requirements from our partners vary based on our own personalities. While some want friendship and loyalty from their partners, others want romance and excitement; some look for a partner they can trust and live with, and others prefer someone they can have fun with. Sometimes, we want our partners to provide for us and to keep us safe; other people want someone to talk to and consult with in their life.

Since we are all different from each other and our needs are all different, it is important that we find the right person for ourselves who understands what we need from life. Relationships can become very happy when we find the right person. On the other hand, if we discover that the person we have chosen to live with does not understand our needs or isn't very interested in fulfilling them, staying with them becomes a difficult chore.

It is lovely to say *"All you need is love"* but the reality is a little more complicated than that. There are many more things that we need from our partners other than love. Actually, the fact that our partner or spouse 'loves' us is only a part of the deal. A relationship cannot work if your partner does not also respect, appreciate, support, and understand you, as well as many other things. Only love is not enough for a happy and successful relationship; everyone needs lots of other commitments from their partners.

What can your needs be in your relationship? Many, including:

—   That your partner is loyal to you.

—   That your partner not only love you, but makes you feel that they love you.

—   That your partner takes care of your physical and sexual needs.

—   That your partner makes you feel physically desirable.

—   That your partner is always mindful of your emotional needs.

—   That your partner is a good parent to your children and takes an active part in their upbringing.

—   That your partner contributes financially to your household expenditure.

—   That your partner helps you in your chores.

—   That your partner maintains a good relationship with your family members and friends.

—   That your partner is attentive to your feelings and thoughts, and always has time to listen to you.

—   That your partner is interested in spending quality time with you without any distractions.

—   That your partner is thankful for your existence in their life.

—   That your partner makes you feel safe and protected from harm.

—   That your partner lets you pursue your own dreams and hobbies.

– That your partner supports your career choice and helps you to succeed.

These are but a few of the general requirements we have from the person we decide to spend our life with. Whether it is our spouse or our partner, we all need our significant others to understand our requirements and try to fulfill them. It is entirely possible that our partner is unable to fulfill some of them since this is an awfully long list. But in a relationship where our partner is incapable of fulfilling most of our needs, or a lot of them – that relationship cannot be a successful one.

There is absolutely nothing to be ashamed of if your list is much, much, much bigger that the generalized one provided here. In fact, it means that you are serious about your relationships and that you are trying to make it work. Having a long list of requirements for your partner to fulfill also means that you are the type of person who understands the importance of hard work in a relationship, and that you are not afraid to try your absolute best to be happy with your partner. To expect a lot from your partner also means that you must be ready to give back a lot, as well!

Whether your partner is aware of your needs and whether they try to fulfill them tells a lot about your relationship. If your partner is unaware of their responsibilities to contribute to your happiness, this could be a very big reason that you are unhappy in your relationship. This is especially true if you are the only one who is trying their best to make your relationship work while your partner is not bothered by its deteriorating condition.

Was There Ever Infidelity in your Relationship?

Infidelity is a big deal in a relationship, and also one of the painful reasons behind some break-up or divorce. Sometimes infidelity is what hammers the last nail to a relationship, something that helps one or both partners to finally admit that their relationship is not going to survive.

Infidelity almost never happens on a void, without a concrete context behind it, except in the cases where one or both partners are compulsive cheaters who have other psychological problems. Yes, there certainly are people in this world who cheat on their partners because that is the person they are. There might be absolutely nothing wrong with their marriage or their relationship, but they will still cheat because of their internal personal issues.

These "serial cheaters" or "compulsive cheaters" will struggle when trying to change their ways; they can be both men and women, but the percentage of men who cheat on their partners without any apparent reason are slightly higher in general. These people cheat on their spouses or partners not because there is something lacking in their relationship, but because they find it exciting or thrilling. These can be occasional one-night stands that they engage themselves in, or full-fledged affairs that can last for years. Compulsive cheaters vary from case to case, but there is one thing that is common in all of them: *most will not stop, even if they get caught.*

In a lot of cases, they prefer to stay in their relationship and cheat rather than get out of it. They will give the defense of a demanding spouse or a partner who doesn't understand them in order to cheat with someone else, but at the same time, make excuses for not breaking up or getting a divorce. There is no winning with a "compulsive cheater"; even when they have a loving partner and a comfortable home to go back to, they will find excuses to cheat.

Other than these "serial cheaters", many men and women in failing relationships come up with several reasons behind their infidelity. As a relationship counselor and a sex therapist, this is not something new to me. Many of the people who come to me for help has been disloyal in their relationship or have been cheated on by their partners. They usually come ready with some good reasons behind their actions as well, as I have found out throughout the years working with distressed couples.

So why do people cheat in a relationship?

Infidelity is not as simple as any of the other problems that couples face in their life together. It is almost never a case of "seeing someone you like, getting to know them better and having an affair with them". While it is of course possible for a man or a woman to meet someone they prefer to be with rather than the person they are with at that point in life, affairs almost never begin for that reason.

The reasons behind cheating for men and women are usually different from each other. In my clinical experience, I have found that what drives a person to cheat can be surprisingly attached to the gender of the person being unfaithful. Also, there are family, cultural, and social influences that mold how a person perceives the faithfulness/infidelity equation.

Some of the reasons I have found in my practice for men to be unfaithful:

–   He simply lies. While he promises fidelity to his partner or spouse, he does not believe in it. This is a slightly different case than a "serial cheater"; while a compulsive cheater cheats because it is a part of the person they are, a liar cheats because he does not believe in staying loyal to one single partner. While society compels them to declare themselves monogamous, they are not so in their heart.

— He is afraid of commitment. Some men fear being with the same person for the rest of their lives, even someone they love and has chosen to be with. Out of their fear of commitment, they cheat with other people, just to tell themselves that they are not bound to just one person for life.

— They are immature enough to think that they are not hurting anyone with their infidelity, especially their partners since they are not aware. This is the reason they give themselves feel better — that no one is getting hurt by their actions; rather, they shower their partners with affection and gifts because they have been unfaithful to them.

— He is insecure about himself and needs other people — people other than his partner — to make himself feel desirable and attractive. Only when other people pay him attention, especially people he is attracted to, he feels good about himself.

— Another version of the previous reason I commonly find is when the man suffers erectile disfunction and want to "test" if he is sexually able to perform with another partner. Interesting enough, in these cases the infidelity has to do more with the man's sexual identity and how he defines himself as a sexual being.

—   Because he has unreasonable expectation from people, especially from people of the gender he is physically attracted to. In his opinion, his needs should be always fulfilled and if his partner can't fulfill them all, he will look for others who will.

—   It can be because he thinks himself superior of others and cheating on his partner is like a reward that he gives himself.

—   It can be because he is not getting enough sex at home from his partner. If they are not getting "adequate" amount of sex (or a specific type of sex) from their partners - which could be because of a lot of reasons - they look outside for sex.

Of course, there are exceptions, but these are the general reasons that men usually cheat on their partners; and yes, a more romantic reason is possible, too. It is entirely possible that a man finds his true love when he is already with someone else, although that does not excuse his infidelity.

For women, in most cases, the reasons for infidelity are quite different than men. Although some women are also capable of being "compulsive cheaters", usually their reasons lie deep within. Generally, when women cheat, it is usually because they are hurting or in distress. For women, infidelity:

- Can occur because they are feeling lonely and neglected by their partners. Communication and emotional attachment are very important parts of a relationship to women; if they are not fulfilled by a partner, women can turn to someone else for comfort. For most women, sex is not just a physical need. Women need to always feel physically close to their loved ones; in absence of that, they'll turn to other people for sex as well as affection.

- Can happen as an act of revenge, especially revenge for their partners cheating on them. In general, women can be vindictive; in some cases, instead of leaving a cheating partner, they would prefer to get even by being unfaithful themselves. In such situations, it is not the affair that is important for women, but the fact that they want to hurt their partners the way they have been hurt themselves.

- Can happen when the woman in question is not getting enough sex, or enough quality sex, in their relationship. Women have just as much physical need for sex as men do; if they are dissatisfied sexually with their partner but doesn't want to wreck their relationship because of it, they might look for better sex outside. These kinds of affairs are more common in relationships that develop for reasons other than love or romance, i.e. when women marry older men for wealth, protection or social standing.

- Can occur when the woman is bored at home. This is one of the biggest clichés of modern society where bored housewives get involved with other people outside their relationship because they are fed up with their life. It can be because they have no career to think of, because their partners don't pay them enough attention, or because they don't have enough commitments to fulfill their day. It can also be because they are actually bored with their partners after a few years together but not so much that they'd get out of the relationship.

- Can occur because of the other person. Women can become infatuated with someone else other than their partner, and the next normal move for them would be to show their interest in them. If the other person is also interested, an affair is likely to develop between them, one that may or may not last. A lot of men and women develop crushes on people other than their partners in a relationship, and it usually depends on the involved people whether or not they want to encourage their feelings.

- Can happen because the woman in question wants to feel appreciated and worshipped. After a few years with the same person, every relationship becomes a little stale, and it is usually the women who feel unloved and unacknowledged. Getting someone interested in themselves is a boost that almost all women crave in their lives, and some of them decide to act on it.

- Can happen because of a low self-esteem. Women with a low self-esteem constantly feel the need to be assured of their worth and can prefer to do so with someone other than their long-term partner. Even when in a happy relationship, some women take the chance of getting involved with someone else who can assure them that they are beautiful, smart, and desirable.

- Can occur when the woman in question knows that their marriage/relationship is over. The decline of a relationship can be because of a number of reasons; a woman starts getting involved with someone else when they know for sure that their previous relationship cannot be saved. It is actually their way of making sure they are not left alone when they finally end their relationship, and that they have someone concrete to help them go through their divorce/break-up.

- Sometimes women crave that certain 'spark' in their relationship – the kind of chemistry that is present in the early days of a relationship. With time, both partners either become busy with their own lives or too familiar with each, resulting in the decline of that 'spark'. This is almost unacceptable to some women, and they look for the chemistry in someone else, i.e., in someone new outside their relationship to get involved with.

- In other cases, it can happen if the woman is mistreated by her partner. This can mean both physical and emotional abuse, where the woman feels insecure, unloved, and unappreciated. Although many women prefer to stay with the partner who is ill-treating them, they also look for contentment outside an unhappy marriage/relationship by getting involved with someone else.

With infidelity, every case is different for every couple. However, there is always some bigger problem lurking behind each case of unfaithfulness. Usually, infidelity is not what is wrong in a relationship, but merely the consequence of something being wrong in the relationship. Infidelities occur in most cases because there are underlying problems in the relationship, ones that do not surface in normal ways. Sometimes happens that men and women cheat because they are unhappy inside, and because they feel trapped in a miserable relationship that is not bringing them any joy.

Is having sexual intercourse with someone who is not your spouse/partner the only way to be unfaithful? Not really! You can be unfaithful to your partner without actually having sex with someone else, by breaking promises or by not keeping agreements (implicit or explicit). Actually, you can unwillingly be unfaithful by doing something that your partner considers infidelity, and you don't.

There are many ways that you can be cheating on your partner or dangerously "playing with fire", even when you are not actually having sex with them:

−	By craving the presence of the person, you are attracted to more than the presence of your spouse/partner.

−	By spending intimate time together, without anyone else present.

−	By flirting extensively with someone else outside the knowledge of your partner.

—   By sharing intimate details of your life that should be only shared with your partner.

—   By inappropriately touching or kissing.

—   By engaging in inappropriate sexual conversation with someone else.

—   By constantly texting or talking to someone you are attracted to on the phone, unknown to your partner.

—   By devising ways of spending time alone with someone you are interested in.

—   By exchanging personal emails or messages with someone without your partner knowing about them.

—   By denying the fact that you are married or in a committed relationship when in the company of someone you find desirable.

—   By lying about your relationship with your partner to someone else with the hope of getting them interested in you.

– By purchasing and giving personal and expensive gifts to someone you are attracted to.

– By talking about your personal feelings and emotions with someone you are interested in; by becoming emotionally involved with them.

– By lying to your partner about your whereabouts or your involvement with a certain person; and many other ways.

It is not only through having sexual intercourse that you can be unfaithful to your partner. Many other acts that are acceptable with a partner is unacceptable with someone else you might be attracted to. While it is completely acceptable to talk about your relationship or your feelings with your partner or your best friend, it is not okay if you get emotionally involved with someone else you might be interested in.

Emotional affairs are actually more common in women than in men; while men, in general, tend to cope with an unhappy relationship by getting physically involved with someone, women become emotionally attached. When women feel lonely and unappreciated at home, they initially look for other people to share their feelings with, a relationship that later can become physical. Men, on the other hand, are more interested in having sexual intercourse with someone else when they are bored with their relationship or having second thoughts about their partners.

If there has been any infidelity in your relationship – by you or by your partner – chances are that the reasons behind it are more complicated than what meets the eye. While it is very much possible for a couple to survive an act of infidelity; over the years, I have seen many couples struggle with their or their partner's infidelity and ultimately, calling it quits. A couple can survive a lot together, but unfaithfulness in relationship is a tough one.

There can be thousands of little problems in a relationship that go unnoticed by a couple, but it is unfaithfulness that manages to break them apart. Therefore, if there have ever been any signs of infidelity in your relationship, remember this: *it is not just the act itself that is disastrous for you, but all the reasons that had led you to them, as well!* You need to focus on the reasons that have caused infidelity in your relationship if you want to get to the bottom of the problem. Ultimately, infidelity is the symptom; rarely is the illness.

Do you have Sexual Chemistry?

Sexual attraction in the first few months is always one of the best parts of the relationship, although the intensity of the beginning almost never lasts for long. Familiarity gives way to intimacy and friendship and the couple in question finds other ways to spend time with each other.

These things change more when there are children involved. When pregnancy and parenthood are in the agenda, it becomes tough for couples to spend some romantic time with each other, with children needing constant attention and the exhaustion that everyone faces. Sexual intimacy becomes something rare between a couple and, in some cases, they get to be with each other only a few times a month or less.

However, sex is an especially important part of our romantic relationships. Almost every couple goes through a dry phase at least a few times in their lifetime – because of pregnancy or children, or a fight or disagreement, or being away from each other, or illness. Even in the most serious situations, a couple need to feel sexually attracted to each other even if they cannot actually engage in sexual intercourse with each other.

If you have not started off your relationship with a strong sexual chemistry, it is difficult to develop it later in your life. Couples who cannot seem to keep their hands off each other in the early days are more likely to keep some type of sexual chemistry throughout the years. On the other hand, couples who are only mildly attracted to each other, or not at all attracted to each other, can be incredibly good friends but almost never reach that state of blissful happiness and passion. There will always be something missing from their relationship without that special chemistry between them.

Think of it this way - sexual chemistry is our body's own way of telling us we are physically compatible with someone. While our mind and heart works in their own ways to determine whether someone is right for us, the body does so as well! When we have an amazing sexual chemistry with another person, it is our body telling us we are physically well-suited with them. It is our body falling in love with our partner's body – to explain it in other words! Since we put a lot of importance on what our heart and mind think about our partner, we should definitely take into account what our body is saying, too.

Although sexual attraction is not the only important factor of a successful relationship, it is definitely a very important one. If your relationship has been lacking sexual intimacy from the very beginning, it can be a reason behind it is falling apart.

Over the years, both inside and outside my practice, I have seen couples who have never gotten over their physical attraction for each other. In my experience, these are the couples who can survive minor hiccups in their relationship because they are still physically connected to each other. Couples who have stopped being intimate with each other are usually the ones who fall out of love; with no physical familiarity between them, it is hard for two people to reconcile and forgive each other for the small problems that are common between a couple.

You can also say that sexual chemistry is the glue that sometimes holds a relationship together. I don't only mean sexual intercourse between a couple, but it is the mere desire to touch each other and stay close to one another that is so important in a relationship. You can see these happy couples around who are always hugging and kissing, holding each other and just being physically intimate, oblivious to the whole world. They seem to take pleasure in just staying close to each other at all times, or as much as they can manage. These are the couples, in my opinion, who can survive almost any obstacle that life throws at them.

To me, sexual chemistry has always been a vital part of a successful relationship. People who are sexually incompatible with each other will find it harder to live together no matter how well-suited they are in other aspects. Romance flourishes on good sexual intimacy, and it is the base of many successful and long-lasting relationships. If you are looking for intrigue, excitement, and romance in your life, you need to be with someone you feel physically attracted to. Otherwise, what sets your romantic relationship apart from any other relationship that you have with a friend or a family member?

The lack of sexual chemistry in your relationship – in present or throughout your time together – could be a big reason behind your disappointment in your relationship. Sexual frustration often leads to desperate acts and can wreck your relationship beyond repair.

Has Love Died in your Relationship?

Ever heard the cliché expression "I love you, but I'm not in love with you"? Unfortunately, this is a valid phase that a lot of couples go through at some point in their life. In other more dramatic words: this is when love dies in a relationship, leaving only a hollow shell behind.

All relationships eventually change. Change is part of the process of growing up and maturing. In a healthy relationship, those changes (although will trigger some sort of crisis) at the end lead to more closeness, deeper and mature intimacy, and a better understanding of the spouse/partner. But other couples actually give up and die at the end. It is not possible to assume at the beginning of a relationship how it is going to end. We all enter into a relationship filled with love, hoping we would feel the same way forever. That is not the case for a lot of couples; they change with passing years, so does their relationship; at the end, some relationships die out altogether.

It is not easy to pinpoint exactly what goes wrong in a relationship in most cases. Sometimes, it is something as drastic as infidelity or a major change that breaks up a couple; sometimes, it is a combination of a thousand little things that makes a person suddenly realize that they are stuck in a loveless relationship. This realization is not easy either! Would you like to wake up one day and realize that you did not love your partner anymore, and that you want out of your relationship?

Yet, it happens to thousands of marriages and relationships every day, all around the world. Although it may be hard to determine exactly what went wrong, you can actually understand if you are stuck in a relationship that is already dead and doomed for failure.

Here are some worrisome signs:

−   Spontaneity will go out the windows in your relationship. You will suddenly realize that the days of "Let's ditch work tomorrow and stay home together" and "Let's go away on a mini vacation this weekend" are long gone from your lives. Life becomes a chore in a loveless relationship, where both members just go through the motions automatically. Never mind dramatic actions, simple day-to-day events like dropping by your partner's workplace for lunch or surprising them with their favorite chocolate also becomes something from the past.

—   Remember the days when you were always holding each other's hands, no matter where you were or what you were doing? Even if you were only at the supermarket for your weekly groceries, you could be seen holding each other's hands. For most couples, this is something spontaneous, not planned. Holding hands indicate something very basic in human beings – the need to physically connect to someone. If you have stopped holding each other's hand – not just in public, but in private too – it could be a sign that your love life has suddenly become very mundane for you.

—   Also goes away the other signs of affection in a couple – hugging, kissing, patting, or cuddling. These are non-sexual gestures that couples use to let each other know of their affection. When these gestures disappear from your life, it could mean that love is dangerously getting cold or somewhat fading away.

—   In the beginning of a relationship, there's never a day that goes by without the loving couple making plans for the future – plans about their life together, getting married or having children, taking a vacation together or getting a pet. Big or small, plans for the future are an integral part of a happy relationship (not every couple that plans together are necessarily happy, but every happy couple have plans together). As love slowly dies, people stop making plans for the future. The reason for this is quite simple: at this point in time, they do not find any enthusiasm in thinking about the future with each other or find it hard to envision a future with the other person in it.

       –   Couples in love are always talking to each other, day and night. Either they are having serious discussions about their hopes and inspirations, or telling each other about their day, their childhood, their pets, jobs, and best friends. Do you remember the early days when you could keep talking to each other throughout the night, about anything and everything that you can think about? Well, there comes a time in relationships when conversations become hard and the television, social media or any other thing seems more interesting than your partner. In my practice I sometimes challenge the couple to have an evening out (to a restaurant, a park, the beach, or even their back yard) and spend time talking to each other; but they cannot talk about kids, work, other people, news, social media post or videos. Interestingly, 100% of the couples ask me with surprise: "Then, what are we going to talk about?!" My answer? "Talk about you, as a couple". There comes a time when couples who could talk for hours about the most mundane topics struggle to communicate, let alone talk about themselves as a couple. That is when you should realize that your relationship is probably dying.

– Are you starting to find thousands of faults with the person you once thought perfect? Even if they had a few faults in the beginning, you knew you could overlook them and still love the person underneath? There are so many things that you do not like – no, loathe – about your partner, and you are not one to stay quiet about them! Well, if you suddenly start getting angry at almost everything they do and don't do, it might mean that you are finally over love's initial rose-colored glasses.

– As much as you loved spending time together in the past, is it becoming exhausting now? Do you always eventually start fighting when you are alone together? If you do not want to spend time alone with each other or if it makes you uncomfortable to be alone with your partner, it is definitely time to admit that the love has gone out of your relationship.

– Does any sign of love of affection from your partner's side make you uncomfortable? Just a simple "I love you" or a thoughtful gift make you feel guilty and undeserving, even angry? It might mean that your feelings for your partner have changed even though their feeling hasn't.

—   Remember those knowing glances, those inside jokes and those special signals that had meaning for you only? Every couple has them; these are actually a significant part of a healthy, understanding relationship. When the love goes out of your relationship, these simple gestures are the first things that you are going to miss between you and your partner.

—   The gap between you and your partner in bed will be growing more and more as you slowly lose feelings for each other. It's not just sex that will be less frequent between you, but just cuddling with each other or spooning in your sleep. The cliché scenes in movies where both partners are lying down as far as possible from each other in bed — that might just be you two!

—   If you do notice problems between you and your partner, you will not be interested in fixing them. Unlike the first few weeks/months of your relationship when you would actively try to mend every crack, you won't be bothered with the problems you are having. The reason is simple — you do not care enough to do so.

–   Finally – and this is an important one! You will be picturing a life with someone else other than your partner. You might have crushes on or "admire" other people while you are in a happy relationship, but this is a different scenario. When you are no longer in love with your partner, you might start fantasizing about a separation and eventually considering leaving the relationship. You might also start envisioning a happier – a more exciting life – with someone else. This usually can lead to an infidelity, because the person has no desire to stay in a relationship where there is no love for the partner.

It is usually a terrible blow when couples first discover they are no longer 'in love' with their partner. Not all people decide to get out when they realize the state of their relationship. Some stay out of habit or because of the family they have together; some stay because although they don't really love their partner, they are still very fond of them. Most couples in trouble find out sooner or later that their relationship has something lacking, but not many of them are courageous enough to take a drastic measure and end their relationships. It usually takes something more than the loss of love for a couple to call it quits, such as one partner cheating or abandoning the relationship.

When you realize that you do not love the person you are with – that is the moment to ask yourself the hard questions. Are you willing to give the relationship a second chance, and seek help to try and salvage it? Is this a relationship worth saving, trying to rekindle the love? Or do you feel the time has come to end your relationship? We all go into a relationship mainly because of love and not just to make our life comfortable; we can face any of the hurdles that life throws at us when we are in love with someone. If it is love that our relationship is missing, what else is there for us to continue for?

We need a lot of things to build a successful relationship – commitment, mutual respect, understanding, trust and compassion to name a few of them. However, it is love that is the foundation of a relationship and without it, no relationship – no matter how much you work on it – can survive!

Did You Settle in Your Relationship?

While we don't always end up with the person of our dreams, it is an entirely different matter when we settle for someone who is obviously not right for us. It may sound incredulous in this modern age of choices and personal freedom, but there are still some men and women who end up settling in their relationship.

Of course, settling does not refer to being with someone who is beneath us or does not deserve us, but being with someone who is entirely wrong for us. This person might be perfectly lovely and right for someone else, but completely wrong for us; but still, we wind up with them because of the circumstances. If that is the case, it is no wonder if the relationship comes tumbling down after a while.

– There are a few reasons that people settle for someone they are wrong for, and the most important reason is that they don't want to end up alone. This is especially true for people in their late 30s or early 40s – both men and women – who are afraid of waiting any longer lest they are left alone without a partner. Sometimes, men and women prefer to stay in unhappy relationships with someone who is clearly not right for them because they are afraid, they will not find anyone else. In other cases, people actually stay with an unfaithful or abusive partner rather than leave because they don't want to be alone.

– Another reason for settling is low self-esteem. When people feel they do not deserve more, they show a tendency to settle for someone who is obviously wrong for them rather than wait for the right person. Women usually have a tendency to belittle their own personal achievements, charm and physical appearance, and think they don't deserve someone better.

–   Sometimes, people settle because they don't really know how a good relationship should look like. Men and women who come from abusive families feel comfortable in abusive relationships of their own because they think it is normal. They do not realize that they are settling as they don't have a clear idea what a happy relationship looks like.

–   External pressure also makes people settle sometimes. These pressures can come from parents insisting on someone because they think will be a good partner; dating someone your friends like, even thou you don't; or being impressed by someone's job, fame or wealth. I once had a client that started living together with a partner, because my client didn't have a place to live at some point and decided it was a good idea to move in together, despite the fact that they had been dating for just 2 months. There could be a million reasons (some very absurd) that people eventually settle with someone they are not sure about.

The reasons may even seem obvious enough to the outsider, but not so much to the person who is actually in the relationship. When you are deep inside a relationship but unhappy, it is hard to realize whether or not you have settled for someone you are not right for. There are, however, some signs that can help you.

– You are constantly trying to change them for the better, starting from how they dress, how they act or who they spend their time with. When you are with the right person, you will not feel the need to change anything about your partner; rather, you will automatically love everything they do. On the other hand, when you are with someone wrong for you, you will always try and change everything about them, mainly because you feel uncomfortable about them.

– You cannot think of reasons you are with your partner, especially after the first few exciting months are over. When faced with the question "What do you see in him/her?" or "Why are you with him/her?" you will not be able to find a satisfactory answer in a hurry.

– You are constantly comparing your partner to other people and finding them (your partner) lacking. It could be a comparison with your previous partners, or a friend, or the partner of a friend you admire, but you will almost always come out the losing party.

– Your partner clearly cares about you more than you do about them, and that is obvious in anything you do. When they do something nice and thoughtful for you, you feel uncomfortable and unwilling to reciprocate the gesture. When they say, "I love you", you either don't want to say it back or feel awkward hearing it.

—   You are always seen making excuses about your partner to others — about everything from what they have said, or how they acted, or even their behavior with you. You seem to be always defending their actions and words to your friends, family members and acquaintances, or you're your mutual acquaintances.

—   You are uncomfortable with being seen with them outside — at parties, work engagements or social programs — because you are always unsure of how they are going to behave. You are especially always worried about taking them with you to your social engagements in front of your friends and colleagues because you are uncomfortable with your partner interacting with your associates.

—   You are more excited about making plans with your friends and work buddies than your partner. You would prefer a fun night out with your own friends rather than stay at home with your partner.

Perhaps the best example of settling for someone who you obviously do not belong with is Homer and

Marge Simpson from television's "The Simpson". If you are familiar with the show, you will understand immediately what I mean! However, their story is one when two very, very unlikely partners are happy together; but that does not mean it happens in real life.

Reality is tough on couples who settle in a relationship despite being obviously wrong for each other. If you see the above signs in your life, it might mean that you too have settled for someone who is not the correct partner for you, and that the relationship could be struggling at some point in your life.

Is there Room for Negotiation in Your Relationship?

Two quite different people come together in a relationship, and it is normal that they will both have different opinions in some matters. This difference in opinion can result in clashes between you, or they can be solved peacefully with proper negotiation.

Negotiations are not only for stern businesspeople and union leaders; negotiations are inevitable between couples with different opinions. Negotiation between a couple can be about something trivial like choosing a movie to watch over the weekends, or something life-altering like choosing the country where they want to settle. There is bound to be difference in opinions in many decisions taken together as a couple, but only that relationship is successful where both parties can negotiate well and reach a reasonable solution.

In many of the couples who have come to me for counseling over the years, I have seen couples behaving in extreme selfishness with each other. In many cases, one person in the relationship will not rest until their own opinion becomes the ultimate solution in every single case; in such situations, the other person has no other option that to agree with their partner's decision every single time. This is not healthy in any relationship, for either both of them. The partner who is always getting what they want is being inconsiderate and dominating in the relationship, and the partner who is agreeing every time eventually will get tired of the situation. This is not how people who love and care about each other should behave in a relationship.

What is more important is that without negotiating with each other, it is almost impossible to find a balance in your relationship. For your opinion to matter to your partner, you have to pay attention to their opinion as well. Even when it is something that is personal and extremely important to you, you need to listen to what your partner has to say about the matter, and vice versa.

Once upon a time – perhaps very, very long ago – the men were considered the masters of the household.

They had the sole right to take any decisions for the good of the family; the opinions of the women were not that important, even when it was their own issue that was being discussed. This was the social norm, and no one minded this demonstration of male dominance over women. Rather, women welcomed this idea of their husbands and partners taking decisions for them.

But this was a long time ago because society is not like this anymore. Today, in every household, both partners have equal say in everything; in a happy relationship, it is both partners who argue, negotiate, talk, and then decide on a course of action – however trivial or serious the issue. In modern relationships, both parties need to have some power. If you decide to win some arguments, you need to surrender at other times.

Consider this: you refuse to go to any of your partner's social gatherings because you don't really get along with his/her friends and work buddies. If that is the case every single time, can you expect your partner to accompany you everywhere you are invited to? Not unless you are a tyrant who bullies your partner and unless your partner is too scared of you! This is definitely not how people should treat the person they love and care about.

If something like this is an issue in your relationship, negotiation should definitely be on the agenda. In a fair negotiation, both partners should have equal say and you need to come to a solution that is acceptable to both of you. If you expect your partner to accompany you to your social gatherings, you have to do the same for them, no matter how much you hate it. That is what partners do for each other – they support each other in their requests even when they do not want to.

Unless you are open to negotiations with your partner, your relationship cannot be a happy and an equal one. You cannot expect your partner to agree with all your decisions blindly without you listening to anything they have to say for themselves. You cannot expect to win every argument and make your decision the final one, even when it is your partner who is right.

– I'll mow the lawn every week if you never ask me to take the trash out again!

– If I do the dishes tonight, I get to choose the dessert after dinner!

– I'll take the kids out for the day if you promise me a lie-down the whole day next weekend!

– I'll babysit the kids when you go out with your friends; but next week, I need the whole evening off to go out with my friends!

This is how fair negotiations look like in a healthy relationship – "I do something for you, and you do something for me!" Both partners win this way, most of the time and no one is left feeling cheated. You must start the negotiation with an open mind and with genuine interest in making the relationship work. If the only thing in your mind is wining the argument and getting the upper hand in the matter, you are definitely not a good negotiator.

Negotiations are an important part of your relationship. If you or your partner is not willing to negotiate whenever you reach a problem, you can never arrive at a fair solution. Winning might feel good at the time, but not to your partner who is obviously tired of agreeing with you every single time. This is the kind of behavior that will lead to either one of you feeling wretched at some point and wanting to quit!

A word of caution: not all negotiations have to be a *quid-pro-quo* transaction. I once had a couple in therapy that entered in some sort of unhealthy "competition" about who did what. Each one kept their own journal of things they did, versus the other person. They even stored receipt of gifts and restaurant bills as "evidence" of how much each one spends, so that the other person "match" the amount when it was his/her turn to pay or buy a gift for the other. In a healthy relationship, sometimes you should just do something for your partner expecting nothing in return; just because you want to contribute to your partner's happiness. As important as negotiation is for the relationship, this should not be the tone of your whole life together.

As the song "Glory of Love" -written by Billy Hill- says, "You've got to give a little, take a little... You've got to laugh a little, cry a little... You've got to win a little, lose a little... That's the story of, That's the glory of love."

When you want out of your Relationship

For your relationship to be a successful one, you both must be as committed as you can to it. It is not enough when one partner is committed while the other person is hesitant and confused. Unlike many other relationships, it is not possible for two people to stay in a relationship unless they are in love with each other and actually want to stay together.

If you are reading this book, I think that it is safe to assume that you are facing some doubts about your relationship. I am also safely assuming that you are thinking of getting out of your relationship at this point. If you have found some (or, all) of the points detailed above in this part of the book recognizable, then undoubtedly there is reason for you to want out.

I'm afraid I have to be a little bold and presumptions at this point, but out of the 12 reasons given in this book, if you can identify at least half of them with your life – you are definitely in a bad relationship. Moreover, if this is the way your relationship is going, it's not a surprise if you are thinking of leaving it. I mean, who would want to stay stuck in a relationship that isn't going anywhere? Everyone deserves to be valued and happy in a successful relationship; as do you!

It takes two people to enter a relationship, but

any one of you can decide at any point that you want to leave. When you are very unhappy in your relationship – so unhappy that you don't even want to try and better it – there is really no other way. Or maybe you have tried a lot to make things easier between you two and failed miserably? It could be either or both!

I have worked my whole life to help couples in distress, but even I recognize that there are desperate cases that arrive to couples' therapy when they are beyond salvage. I personally believe that there is no use being unhappy in a relationship that isn't working, and remain in it, especially when they have a way out. No one should stay in a bad relationship at the expense of their peace, happiness, and even their sanity. Relationships are supposed to be where we are our happiest; where we feel safe and loved. Relationships should bring out the best of us. If we are miserable with the person who is supposed to bring the best of us, what is the use of staying with them?

More often than not, the end of a relationship is no one's fault; rather, it's the two people in it who suddenly fell out of love with each other or seem wrong for each other. Whatever the reason is, it is quite common for a once-happy relationship to fail, for couples who were once very much in love with each other to have a fall out. It happens in a lot of relationships out there; the ones that stand the test of time and reality are those that started working on their relationship from the start, managed conflict in a health way and were both willing to do the heavy lifting.

On the other hand, sometimes the couple does not realize that their relationship is dying, until is too late. So, don't feel guilty if you are the one who wants out of your relationship, while your partner seems adequately happy with it. Remember: *it takes two to enter a relationship, but only one of you can decide to end it.* There is nothing to feel ashamed about if that is the case. It simply means that you are looking for something more in a relationship that your partner is unable to provide for you.

Section II: Walking Away from a Bad Relationship

Even if you are stuck in the worst relationship in the world, it will be difficult to walk away from. No matter how unhappy you are, it is almost impossible to just decide to quit overnight and leave. Unless there is an issue of life and death involved, no one – I repeat, no one – walks away from a relationship, no matter how decaying, without thinking about it a thousand times.

There is no guarantee of success with any relationship. We may all enter a relationship thinking we will "live happily ever after" but it may not end that way. Sometimes, the signs that we are in a bad relationship are unclear. Years of cheating may remain hidden under our partner's lies; years of emotional abuse and jealousy hidden under the title of "protectiveness". Sometimes, the signs are almost invisible – trapped under a feeling of restlessness and desperation. More often than not, the signs are crystal clear, like falling in love with someone else, catching your partner cheating on you or simply having an epiphany that you are in the wrong place with the wrong person. Whatever the signs are – transparent or veiled – the answer is always the same: *get out. Get out while there's still time!*

Even though the answer is obvious, the act itself is not so simple in most of the cases. Whether you have been together 20 years or 2 months, it is always difficult to walk away from a relationship.

Why is it Difficult?

When we enter into a new relationship, we always do it with such high hopes and dreams. Not just that, over the years, we invest a lot in our relationship. We become bound to our partner in so many ways – emotionally, socially, physically, financially, and socially.

Most importantly, we invest a lot of time in our relationships. When we love someone enough to marry them or be with them, we build up a lot of dreams around them. We dream of settling down together one day, buy a house, have children and grandchildren, and to grow old with each other. The end of a relationship means the end of all those dreams together, which is more than heartbreaking.

Besides, there are other important sides to think about: your children, if you have any together. Children are one of the major reasons people hesitate over breaking up or getting a divorce, because they do not want to hurt their children by separating – especially if they are still very young and vulnerable. Couples who are unhappy with each other decide to stay together because of their children in many, many cases; however, this is not always the best decision under the situation. I always believe it is better to separate and stay happy apart, rather than stay miserable together – for your sake as well as the children's sake. Children can cope up fine with divorced or separated parents, more than we give them credit. What they have trouble adjusting to are unhappy parents who are abusive to each other and clearly miserable together. Although "for the sake of the children" is always a good reason for incompatible couples to stay together, it is not always the right decision.

At times, there are some other practical reasons that make separation hard; for example, when you have assets together, i.e. when you run a business together, or own an important property together. Although there are solutions to the problem – after all, houses can be sold, and businesses taken over – it is nevertheless a tough decision to make. Because when you are separating, you are not only selling your property or giving over your business, you are also giving up years and years of joint effort together. The memories of building up something – whether it was your business together or a house you have furnished with each other – are sometimes too much to handle, and especially to let go. Besides, if one partner is financially dependent on the other, this is actually a colossal step to take. The person who is financially dependent will have to think about their livelihood after they have separated, and possibly look for sources of earning.

Sometimes, even when we are the ones unhappy in our relationship, it is our loved ones – our family members, friends, and other acquaintances – that try to convince us otherwise. No one wants to see a marriage breaking, or a partnership dissolving, especially not the people who love us. It is these loved ones who persuade an unhappy couple to "give it some more time", "think it through", "take a trip together", "have a baby" or "spend some quality time together" because they want the best for us. Sometimes our family members and friends become so fond of our partners that they actively try to persuade us to stay together, even when we are clearly unhappy. These kinds of sentiments are more common in certain Eastern cultures and countries, where divorces are avoided as much as possible, not until something drastic has happened to aid it.

Couples who have been with each other for a long time have trouble thinking of a life with someone else. Try as they might, they just cannot imagine life with another person after they have spent years and years with their partner. Without the enticement of a better and happier life waiting for them, it is actually very difficult for someone to take the decision of separating from or divorcing their long-term partner, even when there's clearly something missing from their relationship.

Most importantly, being in an unhappy relationship does not always mean that we have completely started hating our partner. Under years and years of unhappiness, we always care a little about the person we have spent so much time with. Although intellectually we know when a relationship is over, it is very hard to come into terms with it when our heart is doing the calculations. Because we have loved our partner for so long, it is sometimes our heart telling us to "think again", "take a little time" and "give it another chance". The truth is every relationship goes through a number of practice runs before they actually do break up. The promises of "trying harder" and "changing what's wrong" make us give each other chances again and again. No one wants to end a relationship on a whim and regret later; this is the reason even the partner who has been cheating is given a second chance because letting go of a relationship is always extremely hard. We usually wait for something concrete to make up our mind, so that we do not have to regret later that we didn't try hard enough.

We invest a lot of time and emotions on our partners and although the emotions can fade, time is one thing that we never get back. No one is going to live forever, and we have very little time in our hands to do so many things with our lives; a portion of which is spent on our partner. When we let go of our relationship, we are also letting go of all the time we have invested in it – and that is never easy.

Besides, once you walk away or once you file for divorce, it is the end of your relationship. It is not like a lover's quarrel where you can be sure your partner is going to come running after you for reconciliation. If you have both decided on separating, chances are no one is going to try for a reunion, ever. There is not going to be any more declarations under the full moon, and no one is going to come home with a dozen roses or your favorite cupcakes to say they are sorry. That fact alone is hard to come into terms with.

It's no wonder everyone takes a long time to decide to actually leave a relationship; it is one of the hardest things we ever have to do as a person.

How to walk away

It's never the easiest path a person takes – to walk away from the partner they had once loved no matter how unhappy the relationship has made them. More often than not, it takes years and years of planning; everyone constantly questions their decision to leave again and again.

However, if you have made up your mind to get out of your bad relationship, you still need some help with the steps. Don't worry, because in this part of the book, I have discussed a few steps to make this transition easier for you. Read through the next few chapters and you will get a clear idea of what you need to do, and the steps to take to make matters as easy as possible.

Think it Through

Yes, definitely you have thought about your reasons a thousand times. Now, before you make the final decision, think about it the last time: *are you absolutely sure?*

Could it be you are actually making a rash decision based on a sudden round of anger? Could it be that you are actually depressed about something other than your relationship, but confused about it? Could it be that you are feeling disconnected with your partner for some time, and mistaking it for estrangement? Could it be that the problem lies with you as an individual and not your relationship?

There can be a lot of things that are wrong with your relationship that can be improved rather than walked away from. Do not make up your mind to let go of your relationship until you have tried your best.

– Have you tried to better your relationship with your partner?

– Have you tried to communicate with your partner about the problems you have been having with your relationship?

– Have you talked to your partner about what is bothering you in your relationship?

– Have you notified your partner that you are unhappy with your relationship?

– Have you considered your roll in the situation you are living?

– Have you considered all the changes or adjustments you can do to better the relationship?

– Have you tried to view your relationship from your partner's point of view?

– Have you considered your partner's feelings towards you and your relationship?

– Have you tried seeking professional help like couples' therapy?

Most of all, you need to be absolutely certain that this is what you want, because once you take the decision to leave, there's no coming back. This is why you need to think everything through before you act. Once you utter something as final as "This is not working for me" or "I want out", your relationship is going to change forever. Even if you happen to amend your decision, your relationship is not going to be the same anymore.

Plan your Next Move

Before you do anything else, you need to plan your next move, i.e., your plans for the future immediately after you break up with your partner or ask for a divorce.

If you are financially independent, it makes a lot of things easier for yourself. Even if you are alone for the next days, you will be able to take care of your own expenditures. All the separation would mean is a change of address, but you will have your own source of income to support yourself when you are no longer with your partner. The question that arises, of course, is whether that will be enough for you or not. Usually, a couple shares the expenditure for their home from both their income, especially rent/mortgage, expenditure of your children, grocery, and others. All these may not be possible with a single person's salary, unless you can afford them all.

Before you take any step, you definitely need to think about your financial situation first. If you are an earning member of the society, you need to decide exactly what and how much you can afford with your own income. Plan ahead knowing you won't be getting any financial support from your partner. As a single person, you will of course want to move out of the place that you have shared together and look for alternative solutions. If you had been sharing rent/mortgage, you need to figure out exactly how much you can spare for a place of your own and your other expenditures. There are a lot of details to go through depending on your situation, but it is important that you take a thorough look at your financial situation.

If you have been living together - which is usually the case if you have been with your partner for a long time - there is the question of moving out. You will need to think about somewhere you can stay for the time being while you look for a more permanent solution. It can be with your parents, a sibling, or a best friend, but it is always better if you call ahead and give them a heads up. Otherwise, you might end up walking around the town with your luggage at midnight because your best friend is away on vacation.

Other small, yet practical decisions also need to be made before you make a move, like changing your mailing address, cancelling your magazine subscriptions to the apartment you both shared, or replying an RSVP for the wedding of your partner's acquaintance. Although these smaller details are often missed in the heat of the moment, they are nevertheless important decisions that you should spend a few minutes thinking about.

Now, a divorce is a completely different matter

altogether - much more complicated than a break-up. If you are getting a divorce, you need to take care of more details, especially if you have children together. Depending on their age, there will be matters of custody, liquidation of assets, telling your children about your divorce, and then actually filling for a divorce. You might also want to consult a lawyer for the details, but that could wait until you have both come to a decision together. Other family members and friends need to be notified of your decision because in a marriage, they are involved too.

In many marriages, one partner – especially the woman, in most cases – leaves their career behind and becomes a stay-at-home mom to take care of her children. In such families, the mother is financially dependent on her partner. This is also something to consider when you are considering a divorce. You need to decide whether you want to go back to work to support yourself and your children, or whether you would be satisfied with the alimony and child support paid to you.

The best way to deal with everything would be to make a to-do list before you finally approach your partner with your decision. Depending on your situation, your list can look like this:

a. Decide where you are going to stay when you move out.

b. Let that person know so that they will expect you.

c. Pack up a few of your belongings that you need every day.

d. Keep your necessary documents (passports, credit cards, etc.) handy.

e. Keep some cash at hand.

f. Keep your packed luggage close but out of your partner's eyes.

g. Make a list – physical or mental - of all the reasons that are making you take this step in your relationship.

h. Practice what you are going to start the conversation with a few times, and so on.

However, if you are planning on staying while your partner moves out of the house you two were sharing, your list would look completely different. In either situation, a list can be quite handy when the situation arises.

Don't Make the Decision when you are Emotional

Don't take the decision to separate from your partner when you are emotional or feeling vulnerable. This is a very important decision in your life, and you need to make it when you are rational and calm, not mad at your partner. If you are too angry at your partner to think rationally at the moment, leave for a few days until you are calm enough to ponder over your situation. Sometimes, it becomes hard to look at your partner realistically when you are living in close quarters with them; the best solution would be to separate yourself from your relationship for a few days. You can stay with a friend or your parents or take a mini vacation for yourself while you decide what to do. Whatever it is you decide – to end the relationship or to continue it – do not do it when you are fuming mad and angry at your partner.

Let me repeat: this is an important step in your life, too important to end anything in a heated moment – especially if this is a marriage we are talking about. Screaming "I hate you and I don't want to stay with you anymore" in the middle of a heated argument will bring in more problems than you can deal with. Similarly, if you are leaving your partner or spouse because you have fallen in love with someone else, think about the whole thing sensibly rather than emotionally; think hard about what you are leaving behind rather than just looking forward to your new relationship.

Before you take the ultimate decision, make sure you are reasonable and calm, and that your decision to leave your partner is not based on anger, jealousy or temporary depression.

Fix a Time to talk to your Partner

Now that you have made up your mind that you want out of your relationship, the next step would be to talk to your partner about it. Unless you are afraid of your partner and know that they can turn violent and abusive when you raise the topic, the best way would be to sit with them, face to face, and talk clearly.

No double meanings, no false hopes, no sweet talks, no blaming each other, no emotional showdowns; just a mature conversation between two adults deciding their future together. Although almost no breakup is usually this smooth and clean, that is the scenario you should target to achieve while you have one of the most important discussions of your life.

This is going to be a crucial discussion for you, so take note of the following tips:

–   Always do it in person, never via text, email, phone or through a mutual friend. It is not fair on the person you have loved for so long. They deserve to hear from you firsthand and have their say in the matter. However, if your partner is of a violent manner and you are afraid for yourself, or you are too angry at your partner for whatever reason, an indirect approach is certainly understandable.

–   Choose your date well. Unless there is an emergency, don't choose a date when you might both be busy. Do not break up with your partner before an important exam or a presentation, or when they are worried about something in their personal life, like a family member's illness or a work crisis. Instead, choose a date when they are relaxed and free from stress. Choose Fridays or Saturdays, so that you do not have to think about waking up early for work the next day. If you want an effective and level-minded discussion, you both need to be in your best condition.

–   Nights are better if you both work during the day; although, it would be better if you are both not exhausted by the end of the day. Nights are preferable for another reason as well: *you will not be disturbed by unwanted visitor or phone calls demanding your attention when you are in the middle of your discussion.* There is always the chance of someone barging in if it's the middle of the day, especially if you have children. If it is at night, you also have the advantage of extended time in front of you. You can stay as late as you want to without any deadline looming into your discussion.

–   Choose your location well, too. The perfect place for important discussions like these is in the privacy of your own home. Some people choose a public place for breaking the news because they do not want their partner to create a scene - which, if you ask me - is not the right path to pick. Breakups and talks about divorces can turn emotional for both of you, and it is not right to limit them to a public location. Besides, in a public place like a restaurant, there is always a chance of someone distracting you, which can be bothersome.

However, if you are afraid that your partner can turn violent and physically hurt you, a public place may be the right setting for you. In this way, you have the protection of other people you can call for help if things get dangerous. Don't choose a place that you both love, like a favorite restaurant. Choose someplace neutral where you are unlikely to go back again in the near future.

– Keep possible distractions as minimum as possible. If you have children who can come disturb you at any moment during your discussion, start after they have fallen asleep. Better yet, send them over to someone else's house for a sleepover. Keep your phones silent and the television off. This is a time for talking only, and no one should disturb you.

Remember that this is an important discussion for your future; definitely, you would want it to be serious and fruitful at the end.

Convey your Message Properly

Conveying your message correctly is very important; otherwise, you can keep on talking for hours without your partner paying any attention to you at all. If this is not the first time that you have talked about breaking up, your partner may not take you seriously, thinking this is another of your complaining moods. This is why, before you start saying your piece, make sure that your partner is just as serious as you are about the whole thing.

Start the conversation by saying that you have something important to discuss with your partner; do not start talking if you think your partner isn't paying attention and 100% present. Better yet, let them know beforehand that you have something important to discuss with them, via a text or an email. They may guess it's about your relationship or think it's about something else entirely, but they will be prepared for a discussion, nevertheless. Otherwise, you will be home waiting for them to show up, ready with your speech, while they would be out enjoying themselves with their friends, unaware of the situation. Letting them know beforehand will at least guarantee that they will not come home drunk or sleepy.

Wait till you have their full concentration on you

before you deliver your speech. Switch off the television before you speak; you cannot have your partner staring at it while you have something so important to say. Same goes for your phones; no checking emails or browsing Facebook while you talk to each other. On the other hand, a cup of coffee or tea can help you concentrate.

Make your first words count. Your discussion can turn emotional later, so try to express all your feelings well before everything gets too touching in the middle. In the beginning of your conversation, try to incorporate your main point clearly. Instead of beating around the bush with half-hearted dialogues like "I have been feeling restless these days" or "I think something is missing from our relationship", state clearly what you want to say to your partner. Some great sentences in these situations can be the following:

• Our relationship is not working for me anymore.

• I want to break up with you.

• I do not want to stay in this relationship anymore.

• I am not happy with our relationship any longer.

• I am going to file for a divorce because this marriage is not working anymore.

Clearly include the words "break-up" or

"divorce" in your conversation, preferably in the first few sentences. They might seem hard to hear, especially to someone you have loved for long and still care about, but they rule out the chance of any confusion later. Compared to hard words like "break-up" and "divorce", phrases like "take a break", "give each other space" and "spend some time apart" can make things more complicated between you. They may give your partner false hope when there are none; you might be very serious about the breakup while your partner might think of it as a temporary bump in the road if you talk about "taking a break from each other" instead of "breaking up".

Don't get me wrong. There are times and circumstances when "taking a break" or having "time apart" can be healthy, especially under the guidance and the help of a couples' therapist. But this is not what I am talking about here. What I am talking about here is when the decision to leave has already been taken.

Keep a list of your reasons handy (check the previous chapter for this). Otherwise, when your partner asks why you want out, you will be left hesitating and bewildered. Write down all your reasons if you have to and list them one by one after you have declared your intention of leaving your relationship. It is important that you can present all your reasons before things get too emotional for both of you. If your partner interrupts you in the middle, ask for time so that you can finish everything you have to say. A list is important because it helps you to systematically say whatever is in your mind and not miss any important point; besides, it is important that you do not lose track of your reasons while you are in the middle of a discussion. A well-written list can be the guideline you need to help you through the break-up.

Don't be shy of letting go of everything you have on your mind. Do not stop if you or your partner starts getting emotional in the middle; you need to finish saying what you have started. Try to finish your whole speech in one sitting, rather than leaving some for later. That is why I was insisting on choosing nighttime for your discussions, so that you do not have to limit your conversation before you are done.

Be Honest and Firm, but not Brutally So

If you are serious about wanting out of your relationship, be firm about it till the end. Your partner might get emotional and try to persuade you to give your relationship one more chance, but you need to be strong in your decision. Do not give your partner false hope when you have no interest in pursuing the relationship anymore. Do not say you'll try to better your relationship just so that your harsh rejection doesn't hurt your soon-to-be-ex partner.

If you are breaking up with you partner out of the

blue, it can be quite a shock for them, especially if they had no inkling of your feelings before. It is up to you to soften the blow because definitely you don't want your partner to suffer from a bad break-up, no matter how hard things are between you two.

Don't sugar-coat your words because you don't want to hurt your partner; be unyielding and confident if you want swift results. Above everything else, you need to be honest in the message you are conveying to your partner. What you should not do are the following:

—   Do not flatter them by saying something you don't believe. A lot of men and women have the habit of ending a relationship by saying something like "You're too good for me" or "I don't deserve someone as wonderful as you are to me". While these sentences may be successful in softening the blow for the moment, they are usually false. You are insulting both your worth and your partner's maturity level by saying something so falsely flattering. This is definitely a dishonest approach that many people adopt when they are not comfortable with or brave enough to convey the truth.

—   Do not behave like you are doing them a favor by breaking up; this is also one of the most common approaches used by both men and women all over the world. Saying something superficial like "You deserve better than me" or "Trust me, you are better off with someone like me holding you back" is definitely not the honest path to take. Most of the times, a person breaks up because they are unhappy with the relationship, not because they are worried about their partner's worth. To be honest in your break-up, you need to come clean of the real reasons rather than make it sound like you are doing your partner a favor.

— Do not make everything your fault, because that is probably not the truth in your case. In your effort to be nice to your partner whom you still care about, don't end up being too nice to them. Don't say "It's entirely my fault because I am not the right person who can make you happy" or "I can't make you happy because I am not special enough" because you are probably not being truthful about the whole situation. You shouldn't be cruel to the person you are about to break up with, but you needn't be too nice either if it means being dishonest.

— Do not lie to them with a made-up reason for your decision to break up; be honest instead. If you are breaking up because of something they have done, be honest about it. If you are breaking up with your partner because you have someone else in your life, be honest about that as well. Don't end things with "It's not you, it's me" when you had a real problem with the relationship.

However, being honest in your break-up doesn't mean you have to be brutal about it. Also, you can be adamant about your decision to break up without being cruel about the whole thing. Even if there was something seriously wrong with your relationship, you can be honest about it without getting nasty. No matter how miserable you were in the relationship, nothing gives you the right to be cruel to another person.

So, do not end up calling each other names or saying hurtful things that are not true just because you want to hurt the other person. Be kind because you were once in a relationship with this person, and you had a lot of feelings for them once. Just because you are breaking up with someone, it does not mean you have the right to hurt them.

A lot of break-ups turn vicious and cruel when one or both parties try to be honest about their feelings. This can be easily avoided if you are a little careful in the words you choose; being honest does not mean you have to be cruel. You can be truthful about your feelings in a nice sensible way and even part as friends! My husband always says that *giving* someone a tomato is not the same as *hitting* someone with a tomato.

Listen to Your Partner's Side

You might be the one who wants to end the relationship, but your partner must have a few things to say about the matter as well. Do not disregard their emotions in the break-up just because it was your decision. Listen to what they have to say intently; you might end up finding out a lot of things about your relationship that you had missed earlier.

Even when you are completely sure you want the relationship to end permanently, you need to listen to your partner's side of the story. They may have some complaints of their own about your relationship; although it may be too late for you both to salvage your feelings for each other, you can use their tips in your future relationships. Besides, it is definitely better if you know of your own deficiencies and mistakes in your failed relationship, so that you don't repeat them in the next ones.

Remember the following when it is time for your partner to speak about your relationship:

–   Your partner might be hurting after hearing you want to break up with them. If they become emotional when you are clearly not, bear with them. Don't make fun of them for crying or pleading with you to give them another chance. Remember that everyone deals with bad news in their own way. You may be a strong person who can deal with trauma silently while your partner is completely different from you. You need to listen to them sensitively and support them in what they are feeling inside. Be the shoulder they can cry on if needed, but at the same time, be adamant in your decision to end the relationship.

— However, if your partner starts to abuse you or call you names, you won't have to stay and listen to it, even when they are doing so in their pain. Your partner is entitled to their own reactions to the breakup, but you are not required to tolerate it. Ask them to stop and be reasonable if they start to do so or leave the premises until they have calmed down enough to talk to you in a rational manner. Leave immediately if they start behaving this way in a public place or show a tendency to become violent. Ask them to call you or meet you later for a coherent discussion later when they are in a more sensible mood.

— It is entirely normal if you start feeling bad when your partner becomes emotional. However, this does not mean that you should change your mind about breaking up forgetting all the reasons you had listed for yourself. If your partner, in their emotional state, brings up happy memories of your time together, listen to them but do not let your memories alter your final decision.

– Similarly, it is also normal if your partner wants another chance to better your relationship in the future. This is common in most break-ups and the number one reason of postponing a break-up. If you think your partner has a valid point, it is entirely up to you to give them another chance. It is your right to try all resources available to save the relationship. However, if you are adamant about breaking up, this is the time to persuade your partner that you really want to end your relationship.

– Do not be surprised if your partner is trying to manipulate you into thinking everything that went wrong in your relationship was your fault. This is also common in a break-up when your partner is hurt by your decision. If this happens to you when you are breaking up, don't think you are required to stay back and listen to the accusations. Do not let your partner's words get to you and don't let them change your minds. Leave the room if you cannot make your partner stop blaming you or manipulating you; you don't have to listen to them if you don't want to.

Listen to what your partner has to say, but do not let them influence you – that is what you need to keep in mind. The person you have spent so much time with in the past would definitely have something important to say to you, but you need to be careful that what they say don't interfere with your original decision to end the relationship.

Be Compassionate About the Whole Situation

A break-up or a divorce is never the desired outcome of a relationship. When we decide to be with someone we love, we do not see ourselves leaving that person very soon. Rather, we see ourselves getting old together. However, that does not always happen; relationships break up every day around the world even when we never thought they would. It is always sad when that happens, no matter how unhappy we were in that relationship.

Therefore, it is very normal to feel sad after a break-up. You may have been unhappy and feeling suffocated in your relationship, but a breakup or a divorce will definitely make you feel miserable inside. Even when you are absolutely sure you were with the wrong person and that your partner did not deserve you, you are bound to feel gloomy when you finally take the decision to break up with your partner.

The breakup is also going to be hard on your partner, even if they were equally unhappy with you. They might or might not express their true feelings at the time of breaking up, but you need to be compassionate about the whole thing, from the beginning to the end.

- If your partner becomes emotional at the mention of a break-up, take care that you are very understanding and compassionate towards them. You might be feeling relieved about the breakup yourself but your partner might be feeling bad about it; it is important that you show the right amount of kindness towards them. This might be your ex-partner that you are fed up with, but it is important that you end the relationship on as amicable note as possible.

- If you are leaving your relationship because you have found someone else to be with, it is more important to be compassionate in such situations. You might be happier with the new addition in your life than you have ever been with your ex-partner, but that does not mean you have to be nasty about it. If you are leaving your partner for someone else while they are still in love with you, you need to be truly kind and sympathetic to your ex-partner, especially because you will be leaving them in a lot of pain.

- Always be empathetic about breaking up with someone, not just sympathetic. Remember, this could be you someday, walking in your partner's shoes. Someone you have feelings for could break up with you one day because they are unhappy with you in your relationship. If that happens to you one day, you will definitely want the person breaking up with you to be compassionate and kind to you. Treat you partner the same way you would like to be treated if it was the other way around.

Remember that this person is someone you had once loved and someone who had once been a very important part of your life; this was someone who was once your friend, and someone who had once made you happy, even if you are unhappy enough at the present to break up with them. You cannot suddenly turn nasty one day with them because you don't want to be with them anymore; rather it is important that you are nice to them and end everything as amicably as possible.

Don't Play the Blame Game

The break-up could be either you or your partner's fault, but it is no use playing the blame game. You can say what is on your mind about the break-up without blaming yourself or your partner in a harsh language. Just tell yourself - and your partner – that it was the relationship that wasn't working; at this point, neither you nor the person you were involved with is to be blamed for it.

Blaming someone is not going to make the breakup easier. It may help you ease your mind about your decision if you decide to blame your partner about everything that went wrong in your relationship, but in the end – it doesn't matter. If you were stuck in a loveless marriage, some of the blame may be shifted to you for not trying harder to make your relationship work or waiting too long to do something. If you are leaving your partner for someone else because they have not been paying much attention to you lately, you are both to blame under the circumstances.

In most cases, both parties are at blame – if not equally, then some – for everything that went wrong in their relationship. (After all, it takes two to tango.) At the end of a relationship, playing the blame game only increase whatever problems you had between you both. You'll be stuck hours in an argument hurling back and forth insulting comments, screaming "It's all your fault" and "You're the one who has made my life hell" instead of calmly deciding your future. When you are breaking up with someone, it is important that you try to be calm and constructive rather than hurtful and malicious, which is what is going to happen if you start to blame each other for your relationship failing. Besides, what can you achieve by blaming someone at the last minute before you say goodbye to them forever?

Don't start blaming your partner for everything during a breakup, even if it was mostly their fault. If they start to blame you, on the other hand, ask them to stop because it will not help anyone. It is so much better to settle everything cordially and in a mature manner rather than blaming each other!

Don't Go Back and Forth With your Decision

It is normal that you will have to think a lot before making such a big decision of your life. Everyone who thinks of breaking up with a long-term partner or asking their spouse for a divorce will go back and forth with their decision at least a thousand times, weighing the pros and the cons of their resolution. This increases manifold if you have children or other commitments together.

Breakups and divorces are indeed difficult and should not be taken lightly. You need to weigh your decision a number of times before you finally approach your partner with the final verdict. However, my advice is this: *limit all your thinking to before you finally tell your partner what you want; afterwards, maintain an iron will about your decision.*

It is not going to be easy; I'll give you that. No matter how determined you were in the beginning, it is normal to rethink your decision when you have actually faced your partner. It will be harder if your partner becomes emotional or tries to manipulate you or promises to change if you give the relationship another chance. Changing your decision in such situations can only delay what's inevitable, rather than improve the situation.

It is completely okay to want to give your

relationship another chance when you think you have a shot of happiness with your partner. It is not an unprecedented event that relationships have not only survived but flourished, at the last moment. But it is my personal view that you should only change your mind about breaking up with your partner when you personally feel there is hope at the end of the tunnel and you both decide to go and seek therapy as a couple as part of the deal of give it another try. Otherwise, going back and forth your decision just because you do not want to cause your partner pain is not a good idea, because it will barely change the nature and the existing problems of your relationship. All you will be doing is postponing the breakup for the future because you cannot deal with the trauma at the moment.

So, if you have made up your mind about breaking up with your partner, or asking your spouse for a divorce, let nothing change your mind for the moment.

Leaving a Bad Relationship

Leaving a relationship — even a particularly bad one — can be one of the hardest things you have to do in your life. This is a person you have shared some of your happiest days with, someone you have loved and been intimate with, someone who had made you happy at some point in your life. If your life together has suddenly become intolerable enough to make you want to leave — it's still a hard step.

Don't feel guilty if you have been going back and forth your decision a thousand times; or if you've taken two steps back for every one step you have dared to take forward. Breaking up with someone is supposed to be hard, and to leave someone you have once loved one of the hardest decisions of your life. The steps mentioned above in this part of the book may have taken you weeks to complete, or even years! But if you are through them, my best wishes are with you! You have completed one hard part of the breakup procedure, but another harder portion awaits you — the one where you have to deal with the decision you have taken.

Section III: Finding Yourself after a Bad Relationship

If you think you have passed the biggest hurdle by breaking up with your partner, you are sadly mistaken. What comes after the breakup process is the real hard part of the deal, where you have to face your single status – a life without your partner. Whether it was a marriage you have broken out from or a long-term relationship, it is going to be hard to adjust life on your own after being with someone for so long.

The time immediately following a breakup is when people make a number of mistakes – mistakes that can create problems later. Keeping in touch with your ex, meeting them out of emotion, immediately getting romantically involved with someone else – these, and many more, are the kind of mistakes a vulnerable person makes after a painful estrangement with their loved ones. Mistakes like these can stop you from fully recovering from your breakup and from finding closure.

After an upsetting breakup, it is normal for you to be vulnerable and open to mistakes, mistakes that can become serious later. This part of the book is dedicated to help you through your time after the breakup, so that you do not end up making any of the mistakes that you might regret later. Even if you consider yourself to be a sensible person who does not act rashly, you need to give this portion a thorough read so that you don't end up in a difficult situation!

Don't think yourself invincible because you were the one who had initiated the breakup. Rest assured, you will be bothered about the breakup almost as much as your partner whom you have left; you need to take care of yourself, as well. Read on and you will find out what to do and more importantly, what not to do.

Prepare to be Hurt

As I said before, you will definitely be hurt by your breakup, even when you were the one who initiated it. Sooner or later, the pain will come to you, perhaps when you least expect it. You may not expect to be sad if you have come from an unhappy relationship, but you will. The pain can be unexpected to you if you were the one who actually left your partner, but it will be there, nevertheless. Regardless of whether you were in the relationship for a few months or many years, you need to face dealing with the emotions that are going to come to you.

There is no use denying the hurt you will be feeling by ignoring or rejecting it. Rather, you need to come into terms with it and allow yourself time to grieve for your failed relationship. Cry when you miss your partner, even if feel that you hate them at that point; or vent your anger with someone available to lend an ear, like a good friend or -even better- a therapist. What you need the most is to face the feelings of loss and pain that will eventually come to you.

Breakups and divorces are always painful even when you were very unhappy in a bad relationship. Sooner or later, you will be missing the person you used to share so much of your life with. The loss of all the dreams and plans you had for the future with your partner will continue to haunt you for a few weeks or months after the breakup, even after you are over the person. If you don't end up regretting your decision to leave, you will definitely repent all the time you had thrown away on that person, and all the energy you had wasted in a relationship that was doomed to fail.

At the same time, you might also feel guilty about how you have hurt your partner by leaving them, especially if they did not want to break up with you. This problem is more acute in situations where you have left your previous partner for someone new in your life. The guilt can be excruciating when you had been in your prior relationship for a long time and cared for your ex-partner a lot. The pain will come hand in hand with this guilt, and you need to be extraordinarily strong and secured in your new relationship to deal with it.

Getting over a breakup can feel like mourning over the loss of a loved one; it can be just as strong and agonizing. After a breakup, it is possible to feel like you have lost someone very dear to you, like someone you loved very much has passed away. Just like you need time to mourn someone passing away, you need time to get over your breakup. Give yourself as much chance to deal with the grief and the guilt as you might need.

Give Yourself Time

What you need the most for yourself after a break-up or a divorce is time – time for yourself, and no one else. The time after separating from your partner would be hard for you, and you need to set that time aside for you. If you have children with your partner or spouse, they are going to need your support and company, but remember that you need some time apart as well.

There is no limit to the time you might need to get over your ex-partner; it can be day, weeks or even months. You will feel the need to mourn during this time – to mourn the end of your relationship and the loss of the person you had once been happy with. Even when you were in an unhappy relationship which you are relieved to get out of, you will need time to adjust to your new status.

Besides mourning for your lost relationship, this time is also important for you to adjust to your new life – a life without your partner in it. If you have been in that relationship for a long time, your newly single status might seem a little different to you because you were so used to being in a relationship. This is one of the hardest transitions that people have to go through after they have broken up with a long-term partner; they have trouble processing the information that they are single once again. This will definitely be hard for you – that is a guarantee.

It is a completely normal tendency to surround yourself with your friends, family members and other loved ones right after you have broken up with someone; it is also normal to crave intimacy from someone who cares about you. However, the smarter thing to do would be to allow yourself to spend some time alone, to help yourself feel self-reliant. Being with your loved ones might help you feel better, but learning to be alone will help you heal faster. More importantly, being on your own will make you realize that you are an individual who can survive on your own, without being in a relationship with someone else.

Here are some ways to spend your time after a breakup or a divorce:

–   Spend some time doing what you love, stuff you have almost forgotten to do because you were in a relationship. Take an interest in your own hobbies; read a few books, spend an evening alone at home, listen to music that you personally like. When we are in a relationship, we always tend to spend time with our partner, whether we are watching a movie or eating out. No one says you can't enjoy these activities by yourself without a companion! Go shopping by yourself, have lunch at your favorite bistro or catch your favorite movie alone. The main point is that you can enjoy your leisure by yourself, without needing anyone.

— Pamper yourself a little; buy something you always wanted for yourself, something you would not usually spend your hard-earned money on. Take a vacation you have always dreamt of. Go someplace you have always wanted to visit but never had the chance. Take a few days off work to spend travelling around. Yes, alone! You need to learn to enjoy your own company wherever you are, alone at home or out having fun among other people. Besides, there is nothing more soothing to a broken heart than visiting new places by yourself and making new friends.

— Write about what you are feeling in a journal; this will be for yourself only, and no one else. You can address your ex-partner while you write in your journal, or you could just address yourself. No need to send the journal off to the partner you have separated from, or even read it out to your friends. You do not have to worry about your grammar or spelling, or even if your sentences make sense. All you need to concentrate on is to get your feelings off your chest through your writing.

Do this for around 20 minutes every day, or whenever you feel overwhelmed in your grief. This is a procedure that many psychotherapists advice to people who are suffering from loss, indecision, depression, or PTSD, called *journaling*. Journaling could be a huge help in gathering up your emotions and letting them out. It could also be a reminder to yourself about the mistakes not to make in your next relationship, however impossible another one may seem at that moment.

–   Think about the relationship you have left behind. Many people have the tendency to completely emerge themselves in work or their social life so that they neither have the energy nor the time to think about the pain. Although this is an understandable emotion, it is not a practical one. A part of the healing process is to think about your relationship and to express your anger/pain/disappointment the right way. Cry if you want to, or scream, or vent to a friend if that helps – but get your emotions about your failed relationship out of the way.

–   A good way to deal with your relationship after a breakup is to sum it up as if in a story: "Boy meets girl, boy and girl falls in love, boy and girl lives happily together for some time, things don't work out between them after a while, boy and girl drift apart, boy and girl separates." Think of it as a story that you are going to write one day, or a story that you have recently read, or a movie you have watched. Making your relationship into a "story with a proper ending" will also help you get closure.

– Concentrate on a part of your life you have been neglecting recently, because we all do that when we are in a relationship. It can be your career, your friends, your hobbies, or even your children. As you are spending time by yourself, you need to also spend time with the other aspects of your life. Spend more time at work and try to be assertive, take a short trip with friends or drop by to visit your parents and distant relatives, or spend the whole weekend with your children.

It is quite common to miss out on the other people in our lives or our own selves when we are busy with our partner. Now that you are single again, those ignored parts of your life can have your attention once more.

—   Try to do something new that is in no way associated with your ex-partner, i.e., not something that you have planned on doing together. This can be something as simple as taking up a new skill, something as elaborate as learning a new language, or something crazy like sky diving. You need excitement in your new single life, something to look forward to, new friends, new memories and especially, new commitments that does not require or concern your ex-partner. Doing something new is the perfect way to start this new life of yours!

The time immediately following a breakup is bound to be hard for you, but it is also the most important time to heal yourself. Using this time effectively will help you process your grief in a constructive way, and eventually help you get over your breakup. Don't waste this time trying to push your feelings deep inside you; rather, use those feelings to make yourself feel better about everything!

Close the Chapter

A breakup or a divorce means that you have permanently closed that part of your life. After you walk out of a relationship, the best way to deal with it would be to completely stay out of it. After the final confrontation with each other, it is better to put as much distance as possible between you and your ex-partner, so that you can eventually get over the relationship in a healthy manner.

Granted, this may not be possible in many cases, especially if you have children together or getting a divorce from each other. If you have children with your partner, it will never be possible to completely separate from them all your life. You will need to get together to discuss a number of things regarding your children, their interests and their well-beings. Besides, your children – no matter how old they are - will definitely need to see you behave in a civilized manner with each other.

Similarly, getting a divorce will also require you to meet each other a few times, albeit with lawyers trailing. There will be endless discussions regarding your assets and responsibilities, discussions that are going to take a few months at least. Besides, you might have other responsibilities that you share with the partner whom you have walked away from - rent, a joint business, mortgage payment, real estate, pets, social engagements, to name a few. All these responsibilities can make it harder to get a clean break from your partner even if you want it.

However, if the situation permits, try to truly separate from your partner once you have broken up with them – physically, emotionally, mentally, and spiritually. Go away for a few days if you know you will need to face them later; the initial separation in the first few days would do you a world of good. If you can't get away physically, you need to do so mentally and emotionally, at least.

If you do not have any responsibilities that you share with your partner, walking away should be easy. However, it is the staying away that is hard. Most men and women make a few mistakes in the first few days and weeks following a breakup, mistakes that stop them from truly getting over the relationship. Under no circumstances, should you make these following mistakes:

– Call them up just for a chat because you miss them. Remember that the relationship is over and done with, and no matter how much you miss them, you shouldn't call them up just for the sake of talking. It is understandable if there is something important that you need to discuss with them. However, you should not give in to your impulses to check up on them, even just to check if "they are coping all right with the separation" or if "they are too sad about the breakup and not eating well".

– Call up your partner because you have just heard something interesting, hilarious, shocking, or entertaining that you think they would enjoy as well. This might have been something normal that you used to do when you were together, but not when you have separated. This is really something of a habit that you have to cure yourself of, nothing more. Whenever you see or hear something you know would entertain your partner, it is normal that your hands automatically reach for your phone. It will take all your self-control to not do so the first few times, but eventually both you and your hands would get used to it.

— Try and stay friends with your ex because that never happens. Even if you were the best of friends before you got together, your relations to each other changed after romance. Romantic relationships have many more aspects than a simple friendship, including physical intimacy and commitment. It is more than impossible to return to being friends after being involved in a romance with each other. If you have underage kids together, you can certainly remain in good terms; but don't confuse *co-parenting* with *friendship*. It is true that some couples manage to cultivate a friendship after romance, but (and this is a big BUT) in my professional experience: (1) it will interfere with new relationships for both of you, (2) it will drag healing process, (3) both will rarely be on the same page with the "friendship thing" - one can think of the other as a "friend" but the ex-partner doesn't see it the same way (giving way to misunderstandings), and (3) good friendship can flourish only after MANY years of separation. The truth is that after romance you can co-parent, you can maybe have mutual friends, even be business partners (depending on the type of relationship you had). Friendship... that is another thing.

You can try to stay friends with an ex out of sentimentality, but it will be awkward for you and everyone else around you. It is best to say a polite goodbye to your partner and forever close the chapter on that part of your life after a breakup.

−   Take revenge on them; that will be too immature of you. No matter how hurt or angry you were by your relationship, revenge is never the answer. So don't go scratching on their car or sending a brick through their window because you are going to regret your impulsive and juvenile actions later. Not to mention the embarrassment you are going to be in if you are ever caught in the act.

−   Beg them to take you back if they were the one to leave the relationship. Once ended, it is almost impossible to continue a relationship, no matter how much you yearn for it. So, if your partner wants to end the relationship, try to accept that no matter how much you hurt inside. You might want to plead and implore them at that moment, but it will embarrass you later. No matter how hard it is for you, control yourself and don't beg your partner to take you back or to give the relationship one more chance.

– Communicate with them in any form, unless absolutely necessary. This means no funny texts, no forwarded emails, no invitation to parties, no Christmas cards, no birthday wishes exchanged between the two of you. Unless it's something extremely important like mortgage payments or divorce proceedings, stop all kind of communication between you if you want to get over the relationship as soon as possible.

– Stay friends with them on Social Media, on any form of it. Un-friend them on Facebook and un-follow them on Twitter, delete them from your Instagram and on any other Social media sites that you were connected together. Hide or remove the pictures you were together or leave them on; just don't look through them every day. Stop posting on their walls on sending them personal message, because Social Media is also a form of communication, even when it is digital. It's almost the same as talking to them or meeting them when you are friends on Social Media sites. Besides, do you want to see pictures of their lives after you are done with them, especially if they are with someone else?

   —   Stalk them on Facebook/Twitter since that is almost as bad as stalking them in real life. Even when you are not friends on Facebook, you can have some access to their lives, so do not spend hours on their profile trying to make sense of their lives. Don't ask your friends to do the same on your behalf or use your mutual friends' account to peak at their profiles.

   —   Meet them under the pretense of "getting a closure". With a complicated relationship, you will never be able to get the closure you want, no matter how many times you meet. Try to be satisfied with the results you got from your last confrontation rather than meet again and again to get the answers of the thousands of questions you might have. If you have left your partner because they have been cheating on you, let go of the matter instead of confronting them with your queries repeatedly.

   —   Be physically intimate with them for the last time, because that is also a very bad idea. A lot of couples go through this after a sudden breakup; they want to sleep with each other one last time to "get it out of their system". This kind of impulsive action never solves any of the problems, but can make you both emotional and postpone your breakup for a few months. It is therefore better if your last encounter is emotional and verbal, rather than physically intimate. No matter how much you miss being intimate with your ex-partner, do not sleep with them one last time because it will only make matters worse. Besides, I have seen that almost never is "one last time". People will tend to keep going back, not because the relationship should continue, but because of familiarity. The end result will be an undefined link (not a relationship) with your ex that doesn't fit a definition of a couple. Almost always, somebody will get even more hurt.

—   Meet them because you need to "give back their things" or "get your things back". This is usually an unnecessary tact that ex-partners use to meet each other for the last time, often at their homes which can lead to sleeping with each other. Pack all your belongings beforehand if you are the one doing the leaving and leave with everything after the final confrontation. If you did not get that chance, send a good friend to do the chore for you, or bring a friend with you while you get your things from your partner's place. Do the same if you have their belongings at your place – send a friend or ship them over.

Most people make the mistake of meeting for the last time on the pretense of giving back useless and unimportant belongings, which is not necessary. This "final" meeting makes way for further meetups where you can change your mind about the whole breakup. If you are feeling vulnerable and emotional after your breakup, it is better not to chance it because you need to give back an old T-shirt or a few objects.

The time after a breakup is a very sensitive one, where we are often very prone to awkward mistakes. Being a little self-restrained and careful during this time will save you a lot of embarrassment in the long time, and help you get over your breakup better and faster.

Don't Assume the Victim Role

Yes, a breakup is hard; not to mention, painful for both parties. However, that does not mean you have to behave like your whole world has come crashing down and that you have nothing else to live for! Given that is how some people feel after a particularly painful breakup, but you need to remember that your breakup does not mean that your life has ended.

Being single after long years with a special someone can seem a little unsettling. We become so accustomed to our partner's presence in our lives that their sudden disappearance can throw us away from our path. Even when we had genuinely wanted the breakup/divorce, it can seem that way to us. However, behaving like a victim who has just been through a great injustice is simply not the way to live our lives.

It is easier said than done, I know. I really do not want to give out empty textbook advices, but there are a lot of people out there who has been through worse than you. They have suffered losing a loved one or a terrible disease, or financial ruin and never complained or given up. If they have suffered so much and not played the victim card, a single breakup should not be able to keep you down.

So, do not just assume the victim and behave like your whole life is over after a breakup. When brokenhearted, some people have the tendency to believe that nothing good is going to happen to them ever again. They think that they had found "the one" in their life, and that they had let them go; now, there is no one else who can be found to fill that void in their life. This sounds like a defeatist viewpoint to me!

Human beings are not monogamous by nature. If so, no one could rebuild their life after a breakup or widowhood. Monogamy is a decision and a commitment, but once that commitment no longer exists, humans possess the ability to recover in matters of love. You can never know what is waiting for you around the corner; it can be something better than what you had before. Sitting at home because you have given up is not the right way to go. The night is still young and there is something much, much better waiting for you outside your door. So, go out and take a chance!

Embrace your Singlehood

Another mistake that we make right after a breakup or a divorce is to jump into a relationship with someone else, for which the ending is almost never positive. There is a name for these relationships that we get involved in right after we breakup with our long-term partner – a rebound relationship.

Rebound relationships may seem necessary and fun at that moment, but they almost never last. When they do last, it is the exception, not the norm. These are relationships we jump into because we are either not accustomed to being single and by ourselves, or because we are looking for a change after being with the same person for a long time. Either ways, these rebound relationships are forged in a hurry with the first person who interests us after a particularly bad breakup or a painful divorce.

Getting into a new relationship immediately after leaving the previous is one of the biggest mistakes we can make. It is important to live a single life for at least some time. When we have been with someone for a long time, we almost forget how to be single. It is very important that we spend some time in our company and learn to enjoy ourselves. This is one of the most crucial parts of growing up and getting over our painful breakup.

As I mentioned before, it is important to spend some time by yourself doing the things you personally love doing. Not activities you used to enjoy as a part of a couple, but hobbies and favorite pastimes of your own. Instead of immediately looking for another love interest, it is important that you enjoy being single and unavailable for a while. Not everyone needs to be with a loving partner to enjoy themselves; you can have fun by yourself or with other people in your life.

After a breakup or divorce you have a unique opportunity to get to know yourself; get to know who you are outside the context of a relationship and who you are after the relationship experience. To help you advance in knowing yourself, try to answer these questions:

- What have I learned from this ending relationship?

- What have I learned about myself throughout this experience?

- What areas of my life need special attention?

- What changes I need to embrace?

- What positives I reaped from the past relationship?

- What are the pains and hurts I need to deal with now?

- What I really want to do at this stage in my life?

The most important thing is that you take some time out to be on your own instead of being tied down in another relationship. This means that you should not be looking for someone special to get involved with as well; you need to be just enjoying your days as they come instead of worrying about "finding someone to spend the rest of your life with". Look at it this way: that "someone special" is you. No matter what age you are – in your early 20s or in your late 50s – do not stress about a looming deadline for your chances of finding` someone else. That thought needs to stay away from your mind while you get comfortable with your single life.

No, this does not also mean that you have to be bitter about all romantic relationships in the world and vow to be forever alone. Every notion you might get of "I never want to fall in love with anyone in my life" or "I'm better on my own; I don't need anyone to make me happy" cannot be good for you. I'm not asking you to give up on love entirely; I am just asking you to give yourself some time before you look for "the one" again. You shouldn't give up on romance entirely because you've been burned once; you just need to wait a little to heal yourself before you make that plunge again. More importantly, you need to give yourself some time to love yourself before you are ready to love someone else!

Being single can sting a little when you are surrounded by other happily-together couples. It can sting you on the weekends and on the holidays when everyone is busy with their significant others and you are streaming your favorite TV series on Netflix. It can definitely sting when you don't have a date for a wedding or a formal social engagement. But look on the bright side: there are other people in your life who love you and want to spend time with you. Give them a chance to make you happy instead of always relying on romance. Pay attention to the other aspects of your life for some time instead of browsing for a soul mate.

Take your time to be happy with yourself, and the person who is absolutely perfect for you will come along when it is the right time. For the time being, embrace your singlehood with as much aplomb as you can!

Keep the Good Memories

The breakup or the divorce may leave you emotionally drained and screaming for the hills, but they should not be the only reminders of the entire relationship for you. Even if the relationship was very bad for you at the end, you must keep remembering the good times you had with your partner in the early days.

Of course, there must have been some good times that you had together in the beginning - the days when you were newly in love and crazy about each other. Maybe those times were ancient history by the time you have decided to separate, but it is important that you keep those memories alive inside of you. Otherwise, it might feel that you have only wasted your time and energy on a failed relationship without getting anything in return.

Your good memories are your reward for the relationship you have invested your valuable time and efforts on, even if it has ended. Without them, you have only the bad memories and the heartbreak left, and those are enough to make you feel bitter. Remember only the bad bits and you won't have the courage to look forward to another relationship after the one that has failed and made you feel miserable. Most of the people who have suffered heartbreak have the tendency to look only at the bad memories, and this makes them sigh away from another chance at romance.

Immediately after the breakup, maybe you are going to feel that you hate every single part of your ex-partner. Maybe you are going to hate the very thought of them, getting angry every time you hear their name, and much more. This phase does not go on for long, thankfully; because hating someone so vehemently for long will leave you exhausted inside. You might want to curl up and go to sleep for a long time so that you will not have to feel this way, which is completely normal. However, you will start feeling better eventually, and that is the time to concentrate on all the good times you had as a couple.

As you start getting over the breakup, the memories will come back to you and you will actually find the strength to reminiscence over them without breaking down. However, if you concentrate on the bad memories only, you will end up feeling bitter inside. Focus only on the reasons you decided to quit, and you will never find the courage to fall in love with anyone again. So, learn from your bad experiences, but do not let them be the only thing you remember from your relationship, even when they were mostly what you remember from that particular relationship.

The good memories, on the other hand, will help you heal better. The memories from all the good times you have had together as a couple will remind you that you didn't completely waste your time on your partner. This can actually be good for you, because you won't have to shy away from the relationships in your future because you are absolutely sure they are all doomed to failure as well.

However, it is important to remember not to romanticize too much about all the happy memories you had with your partner. Just as we have the tendency to focus only on the bad memories, we can also hang on to the good ones, and idealize them into something more than they were. Over time, we begin to consider a great vacation to an exotic country with our partner "the best time of our life"; we start to think of them as "the most romantic person in the world" just because they have given us a thoughtful gift once. This kind of attitude can definitely be harmful, especially to your future relationships.

How? Because if you romanticize your past relationships and partners too much, you will start to compare them with your present partners. In most cases, your present partners would come out the losing party because you have put your past relationships at such a high pedestal, no one – even someone who is better suited for you – can reach it. A perfectly normal relationship can become the happiest time of your life because you romanticized the good memories too much. This is just like we tend to turn ordinary people into saints after they pass away; we overemphasize their good points until they become absolutely perfect in our minds. People whose partners and spouses have passed away prefer to live with their old memories rather than be with someone more suited to them, because they idealize the relationship they had before and nothing else can get near them in quality.

After such a "perfect" relationship, is it possible to settle for something regular?

So, remember the good memories instead of only focusing on the bad, but do not idealize them so much that nothing else can come close to it. Both tendencies are wrong, and most importantly, harmful for all the relationships you might have in your future.

Live in the Present

The time immediately after a breakup or a divorce is when you need to live in the present. Not thinking back on the past or wondering about the future, but just enjoying the present. This is not the time when you need to think back on the mistakes of the past – what you could have changed or done better, or what wrongs you could have not made. Neither is this the time to wonder if your future has something good in store for you! What you need to do is to live each day as it comes to you.

No, it is definitely not going to be an easy task, in the middle of all the pain and the heartbreak. The last thing you'd want to do is to live in the present. Like most people suffering from a heartbreak, you would want to wallow in your grief and look back on the past, wondering if you could have done something different. Worse, you would want to contemplate your future as a single person and wonder if you will ever find someone else to love in your life. You will want to do anything but live in the present!

However hard it is, here are some ways that you can introduce some positivity in your life.

—   Be grateful for where you are in your life. Even when you are hurting inside from your breakup, remind yourself that you have made the right decision. Try to look at your single life in a positive way, however hard. Remember that you have taken this decision because you thought it the right one. Although it hurts you to stay away from your partner, be grateful that you had the farsightedness and the courage to take the decision.

—   Surround yourself with positive people, especially people who understand and support your decision. There will always be some people in your life who would urge you to give your relationship another chance, usually in case of a divorce or a long-term relationship. It is easy for you to be influenced by their insistence, especially since you will be in a vulnerable state yourself. You don't need such people around you during this sensitive time, no matter how close they are to you. What you need, instead, are good friends who know and understand what you have been through and support your decision.

— Do what makes you happy, as opposed to what you used to do to make your partner happy. If you had minimized eating out because your partner preferred home-cooked meals, start trying out new restaurants with your friends since you like to. Similarly, if you had watched sci-fi movies to keep your partner company on your outings, take time to watch the kind of movies you like as a person. Instead of automatically going back to activities you enjoyed as a couple, or activities you participated in to please your partner, do what you feel like yourself and you will eventually feel more positive in your life.

— Think of all the other aspects of your life that are still very important to you; your children, if you have any, your career, your friends, your family. Just because you are not in a relationship anymore, it does not mean you have nothing else of importance in your life. Concentrate on what you do have in your life, and they will make your feel more positive about your surroundings.

–   Make at least one positive change in your life. It can be to start exercising or to eat better, or to concentrate more on your career/education; you can even start taking new courses or move to a better location. It can be a small or a big change, but it needs to be something that has a profound effect on your life, and definitely a positive one.

–   Think "Don't cry because it's over; smile because it happened". Even in your pain, remember the good times you had with your partner and be grateful for them. Think back on all your positive memories of the relationship instead of only the bad ones. If you can think of your failed relationship in a positive manner, it will help you look at your own life positively.

Above everything else, you need to view yourself and your life in a grateful light. Instead of wallowing in your grief and thinking your life is over, think of your future optimistically. Your present will start to look optimistic when your past and future becomes positive.

Know the Right People to Talk to

It is completely natural that you'd want to talk and unburden yourself after a breakup or a divorce, but it is important that you talk to the right person. You will be in a vulnerable state after such a trying time in your life, and you will not want to talk to someone who misunderstands you or makes a different meaning of your words.

Definitely, you need someone who is close to you, someone who loves you and understands you, and won't judge you for your actions. In your vulnerable state, you need the company of someone who will be kind and considerate to you even if they do not agree with your decision. Most importantly, you need someone who will listen to you but will not share your story with others without your permission.

Your best friend(s) is obviously the right answer; friends are the best when it comes to talking about breakups and heartbreaks. They will listen to you for as long as you need to talk and heap tissues on you, in case you need to cry (they can also be a good source of comfort food.) What is more important, however, is that with your friends around, you won't have the chance to make the mistake of calling up your ex and begging them to take you back.

With your real friends, you can talk, cry, scream or vent, and they will listen to you, even agreeing. You can be honest with them and they will not judge you; they'll even support you when they don't agree with your view. They will be the first ones to agree that you deserve much better than the person you have just left behind, and that your real soul mate is just around the corner.

However, it is preferable that you do not choose a mutual friend to vent. That particular person, if they were friends with you both, may find the situation awkward. They might not want to choose a side between you two and be stuck in between. With a mutual friend, you can find it hard to talk, because you cannot be sure whether what you say in private will be repeated to your ex. Besides, can you be sure that same friend isn't being the confidant to your ex-partner as well, hearing their side of the story and agreeing with them as well? For these reasons, it is preferring to choose an exclusive friend of your own rather than talking to someone who is a mutual acquaintance.

It does not have to be a friend who you talk to for unburdening yourself; it can be anyone else you are close to around you – a colleague, a sibling, or a parent. It might seem almost surreal to share our romantic saga with a parent, but they can be a surprisingly good source of wisdom and knowledge. They have been through a lot in their lives, and they can help you through with their experiences. Even when your parents are alien to heartbreaks, breakups, and divorces, in most cases they will definitely know the right things to say to you in your grief. Sometimes, a loving parent is what you need more than an understanding friend; parents will love and cherish you no matter what situation you are in your life, and they will shower you with attention and concern - which is sometimes what we need the most.

Siblings, cousins, colleagues can be trusted to be kind and considerate during this trying time as well. They are your well-wishers, and they will help you through the pain you are feeling. A large group of loved ones are sometimes what you need to get you going, to have fun and to take your mind off things. Surround yourself with people who love you when you feel the need to talk, and you will get through your heartbreak more easily than you thought possible.

Whatever you do, do not show off your grief on Social Media sites via sad lyrics and depressing quotes. There's absolutely no use making your personal life public on Social Media, for others to judge and/or laugh at you. Believe me, that is what most people do to these public declarations of heartbreak! Your relationships, as well as your breakup and divorce are personal issues that you need to solve on your own, in private. Only a few loved ones need to know the gruesome details of your heartbreak, not hundreds of acquaintances on Facebook!

Always know the right people to talk to when you are feeling down, especially after a breakup or a divorce. Your closest friends, your parents, your siblings and close cousins, colleagues who are your friends – these are the people who want the best for you, not strangers and acquaintances off the street. Talk to the right people and they will know the right ways to help you. Talk to the wrong people and they will make you feel worse than before and send you back into a never-ending depression!

Don't Wait for Closure

It definitely is nice to get a proper closure at the end of a relationship, but not everyone is that lucky. A lot of relationships end badly without any chance of closure between the couple; you may end up not even having the final discussion with each other.

Do not wait for your partner to provide the closure you need. Many people, after the breakup, look for ways to communicate with their ex-partners, only to worsen the situation more. Most stories of stalking come from people hounding their ex-partner for a closure; besides, you could end up getting back together looking for closure in a relationship you had willingly left behind.

First of all, you need to understand completely what closure is. Closure in a relationship is when both parties understand the real reason they are breaking up and can walk away from each other with peace of mind, as much as is possible under the circumstances. The ideal closure is when both have found all the answers to the "Why's" "How's" and "When's" in their relationship. It does not mean you will be magically healed and welcome the breakup with open arms, but it simply means that you will be better equipped to deal with the breakup.

Such kind of perfect closure is rare in a breakup, and it is not a good idea to look for it. If your desired closure does not come from your partner, it should come from within you. In situations where you and your ex-partner are not communicating after the breakup or divorce, here are some ways you can achieve it.

— Try writing a letter explaining everything you have been feeling about the relationship and the breakup. Fill it up with everything you wanted to discuss with your partner when ending the relationship, but could not — everything from your pain, disappointment, grief, and discontentment. The letter can be as long as you want it to be, without having to worry about your ex-partner reading it.

You can send the letter to your partner, or not — that is completely up to you; or, even better, you can burn it or tear it into a million pieces. If you happen to send that letter to your partner, you cannot spend another minute thinking about them reading it. What happens to the letter should have nothing to do with you; you should not care whether they read it or not, or what their reaction to it was. If you decide not to send it, the same theory applies. Writing and destroying that letter will be your last action in that relationship; you should not think about it anymore.

– Remove all your partner's personal belongings from around you, even things you have collected together. Send them back to your partner if they are important belongings but do so via a mutual friend or an acquaintance, or a professional delivery service. It is better not to engineer a final meeting alone in someone's house just to return each other's personal belongings. If there are some things your partner doesn't need back, throw them away or give them away to charity instead of keeping them around.

If there are some expensive or precious items that you have brought together that you neither want to return nor throw away, keep them hidden from view for the moment until you are over your relationship, or keep them with a friend for safekeeping.

– These days, it is not easy to throw away the memories of your good times together; especially through Social Media, it is possible for you to come across some old photograph or memory of you two together. To avoid such situations, it is important that you keep away from these Social Media sites for the first few days/weeks/months that you are grieving. Remove or hide all the pictures you have of each other online, and un-tag yourself from your pictures on your ex-partner's account. Blocking each other from these sites will also spare you intimate knowledge about each other's life that you don't need to know.

–   A burning ceremony might be a good idea for a closure. As juvenile as it sounds, it is sometimes a refreshing change. Tear a stack of your photos, a letter you have written to your ex, and a handful of inflammable souvenirs like love notes or emails, or tickets to a show you have seen together, and set them on fire. This could be a private burning ritual by yourself, or something that you do with your friends. However, you need to be careful since you are literally playing with fire here. You don't want to burn down your house when trying to get a closure, do you?

–   If it is possible, a change of scenery would do you a world of good. If you are the one who has walked out of the relationship, it will be easier for you to move into a new apartment or a house that has no memories of your ex. After a particularly bad breakup, many people choose to move to a new city or even a new country to get away from the memories. If this is not possible for you, moving into a new building in a new neighborhood may help. At the same time, you will have access to new restaurants and grocery shops that you have not visited with your partner before and therefore, have no memories attached to them.

–   If changing your apartment or house is not an option, try changing the décor a little. Choose a different color scheme for your interiors, something that is a complete change from the previous color. If possible, replace a few crucial furniture around the house as well - your bed, for instance, or your couch; mainly furniture that hold a lot of memories for you. This can be a project to take your mind off things as well as a positive change for you to concentrate on!

–   Sometimes, when you can't be satisfied talking to a close friend or a family member, talking to a professional can help. Although not many people visit a counselor for getting over a breakup or a divorce, a psychotherapist can certainly help you move forward and leave all your baggage behind. If it agrees with your beliefs, you can also seek help with a spiritual advisor like a pastor, priest, or rabi.

The perfect closure is hard to come by, even harder if you wait for your ex-partner to provide it for you. Only a few breakups and divorces end up amicably; the rest almost always has a confusing ending. The right closure is an inside job. Only you can provide the right closure you need to get over the relationship, so do not wait for your partner for it.

Put Yourself First

I have mentioned this before, but here it goes again: *always put yourself first.* When in a relationship, we have a tendency to put the need of others before ours – our partner's, our children's, our friends, our pets, our in-laws, and many others who are important to our life together as a couple. This is a change that will not come to you easily, especially if you are the type of person who lives for their family.

There are many people around us – of all gender – who put others needs above their own. They let go of their own needs and desires to satisfy their partner's and children's requirements. A breakup or a divorce is the perfect time to start thinking about yourself and not of someone else. You need to put yourself first and above everyone else and think about what you want from life – not as a parent, a spouse, or a partner, but as a person.

You need to spend time and effort on yourself, not to mention your hard-earned money on something you want for yourself. In other words, pamper yourself in ways you never would normally. Do what you like by yourself, with no one in particular to accompany you; shop without anyone to criticize your choices. Start eating better and healthier, exercise more and get your life back on track. Be around people if you feel like it, or alone if you are not in the mood for company. If you can't find anything to do for yourself, go to sleep and give yourself some much needed sleep.

Spend more time offline doing real stuff rather than online looking at your friends' lives. Social media sites, where you get to see happy couples at their best, are not the best place for you immediately after a breakup. Do something more real like reading a book or watching a favorite TV show; binge on your favorite TV series or play your favorite tunes on high volume.

Above all, make sure you are spending your time for your own amusement, and not to entertain or accompany someone else. Think of what you want to do during this vulnerable and trying time of your life and do them. For once in your life, think of yourself first and others later!

We often let go of our own life goals in order to cater for our partner's and family's needs. Women do this all over the world more than men; they let go of their own career and passion in life to become an involved partner, spouse, or mother. Not only women, but some men are also known to put a stop in their own purpose in life to become a responsible partner, spouse, and father. This kind of sacrifice is common in men and women all around us – for each other and for their children. Although it may be too late to completely turn your life all around at this point in life, a breakup or a divorce is the perfect time to concentrate on what you had sacrificed for your loved ones many years ago. This is finally the time to put your own needs before someone else's, and to realize that your life goals are also as important as anyone else's.

It could be a passion in music that you had left behind to pursue a more responsible career, or a promising aptitude in art, drama, or sports. You do not exactly have to forsake your day job to take up your passion again, but you can concentrate on what was your passion in your leisure. The time that you had spent on your partner can now be spent doing what you had always loved but given up eventually. It could be anything that attracts you, as long as it makes you happy. Remember: the main thing is that you get to live for your own and determine your own life purpose for some time!

Learning from your Bad Experience

A breakup/divorce is nothing more than a life experience that teaches us valuable lessons for the future. That is the best we can do from our bad experiences – gain insight, learn and, hopefully, not to make the same mistakes again. Whether you were in a relationship with a terribly bad person or there was something always missing from your relationship, there are a lot of learn from your bad experience.

So, what can you learn from your failed relationships that will help you to be more successful and stable in your future romantic endeavors? Well, a lot really!

- First of all, we must remember to enter the relationship for the right reasons. To get involved with someone for reasons other than love and romance is basically signing on its own expiration date. To be with someone because we are only physically attracted to them, or to be with someone because they have more feelings for us than we have for them, or to get involved with a person because they have everything we think we need – these are all the wrong reasons for a relationship.

We should be only with the person who we love and cannot imagine our life without, and not because they look good on paper and because we are ready for a relationship. One of the biggest mistakes we can make is to get involved with someone based on their physical appearance, their status in life or their other merits, and not because we are in love with them. Entering into a relationship because of the wrong reasons almost never means 'happily ever after' and we shouldn't be surprised when these relationships come to an end.

• Also important is the power of sexual chemistry in a relationship. No matter how much we love someone or how perfect they are for us, if we are not physically compatible with our partner - that relationship is not going to be a happy one. Sexual chemistry is just as important – if not more – as any other emotional and mental compatibility we can have with our partner. If you are initially not sexually attracted to the person you are getting involved with, chances are slim you can develop a chemistry later and salvage the relationship.

• Do not go into a relationship thinking you can change the other person. No one profoundly changes who they are on the inside, to please the person they love. So, if you are getting involved with someone who is irresponsible and careless with money, they are probably going to always remain so no matter how much you try to change them. If you are marrying someone whose eyes always stray towards other people, you are definitely going to have to be careful all your life. So never assume that you can change your partner once you are together; only get involved with them if you are completely all right with the person they are on the inside, because chances are that they are never going to fully change.

- Friendship needs to be the base of every relationship, even the most romantic ones. Beside love, commitment, stability, and sexual chemistry, it is important that you are friends with your partner. Being friends with each other means that you can talk to your partner about everything and anything, that you can share all (almost!) your secrets with them, and enjoy each other's company at all times, doing what you both love. Being each other's friends will give your relationship stability and durability like nothing else in life.

- Do not go into a relationship hoping it will solve all the other problems in your life. Being with the right person can be a magical experience; but if there is anything lacking in your own life, you are the one who has to solve it. The right partner will not be able to magically fix everything in your life, so do not enter a relationship expecting so.

- Your partner/spouse may be the most important person on your life, but they will not "belong" to you. All the nonsense you hear about "belonging to each other" should not be taken literally; no one in this world can truly belong to someone else, only themselves. Commitment does not mean that you have to surrender your personality and your individuality to another. When you are with someone, you have no right to control their thoughts and actions, and neither do they. Do not think you will be able to control your partner's actions when you are in a relationship, no matter how devoted you are to each other.

- Always enter a relationship being your own true self; do not change yourself too much to please or placate your partner. We can only do so for a few days or weeks before we turn back to the person we really are on the inside. You might want to showcase your docility when you are a party-person inside, or a responsible facade while you are wild and negligent inside, but these facades will not last forever. Sooner or later your partner will find out the person you really are, and you would have started off your relationship on a fib. You would not want that, especially if you are serious about your relationships. Although it is quite normal to show our best faces during the early stages of a relationship, the face you show should not be too far away from the truth of who you are. You don't want your partner/spouse to get a nasty surprise after a few days, do you?

• Do not expect your partner – however magical they seem to you – to "complete" you. Those kinds of romances are actually fables portrayed in movies, books and love ballads, but in reality, the only person who can "complete" you is you! Your partner can certainly make you extremely happy and fill your life with joy, but don't depend on them to make sense of your life. In these modern times, our relationships are only a part of our lives, albeit an enormously important one. We need to focus on the other aspects of our lives as well to be content – our careers, our success, our friends and family, our ambition and goal in life, our dreams, and hobbies. Only a relationship, even an incredibly good one, cannot complete our lives no matter how much we rely on it.

• Never underestimate the power of communication in romantic relationships. After the initial flurry of romance, "getting to discover each other" and sexual attraction are over, life can become a little dull for you both if you cannot communicate with each other. It is very important that you are able to talk to the person you are with and share your thoughts and ideas. Remember not to be too serious about someone you cannot really talk to. If you want the relationship to last beyond the initial stages, you need to be able to communicate effectively with the person you are going to spend your life with.

• Do not go into a relationship expecting it to last forever! It may seem harsh to you, especially in the beginning of a new romance when everything seems perfect and delightful. It will hurt you even more when the romance that you thought would be forever fails; if you go into a relationship knowing that it could come to an end one day, the pain may be a little less if it actually does. However, that does not mean that you need to enter every new relationship with a negative ending in mind or give up trying at the first signs of trouble, of course! There are a million examples of "happily ever after" around us that could be our inspiration. All I am saying is that you need to remember that the relationships you are entering is based on the desire of both partners to be together and could not last forever. This means that you both need to work on nurturing the new relationship; on the other hand, if the relationship doesn't work, you will have the courage to be strong and decisive when you need to be.

• Always know your boundaries and your deal breakers when you enter a new relationship. Never, under any circumstances, do something which is unimaginable for you because of your partner's insistence. Never compromise on your own morals and ideals even when they are for the person you love the most in this world. If you do break your own ideals because of your partner, your own betrayal will come back to haunt you sooner or later. Be clear about what you can and cannot do in a relationship and be sure to let your partner know about them. There are some aspects of all of our lives we should never negotiate with, and they should also be present in our romantic relationships.

- Always remember the importance of "me time" in your relationships. Of course, you'd want to spend every waking moment with the person you love, but it is also important that you spend some time on your own or with other people doing the things you love. There's a whole chapter on this topic in the first part of this book that you can go through again, but remember to invest in your "me time" instead of doing everything together.

- If you stick to a relationship long enough, it is bound to change and you need to be okay with it when it happens. You cannot expect to be the same couple doing the same things year after year. Time will change you both, as will the added responsibility of mortgages, children, friends, and family members. If you expect to remain stuck where you first started together, it will only mean pain and disheartenment on your behalf. So, before you enter a new relationship or get too serious about it, know that it will eventually change with time.

Do not let the failed relationships of your past ruin your future romances. Always believe in your own strength to cope and make the right decisions when the time comes. Love is a wonderful emotion a human being can experience in their lifetime, but it is always important that you keep a cool head on your shoulders and do not get too carried away by your romance.

I know that some of these things are easy said than done. But never forget that you have the power to make decisions that will impact your future in a positive way. Do not be too overwhelmed, too fast or too blind when it comes to a new relationship; rather, take your time. Relationships can be wonderful when it is with the right person and good things come to those who wait! So, wait a little before you fall in love the next time.

May your future be filled with all the wonderful things love can bring!

Conclusion

"Bad Love: *Identifying and Getting Out of a Bad Relationship"* is not just any other book for me, but a project close to my own heart. This is a topic I have researched, thought about and worked with for many years and I genuinely believed it necessary.

As a therapist working with couples for more than two decades, I have mixed feelings about some relationships. While I believe love to be one of the most beautiful experiences a human being can go through, I have also seen the heartache in the distressed couples I have closely worked with.

"Bad Love: *Identifying and Getting Out of a Bad Relationship"* is, regrettably, not about the flourishing relationships that we see all around us; rather, it is about the unsuccessful and bad relationships that we have all more or less faced in our lives. Sometimes, we know straight away when our relationships go wrong, but sometimes it takes us a long time to figure it out. Sometimes, it is easy for us to walk away from our relationships, while at other times, we have to spend hours of sleepless nights tossing and turning in bed.

Whether we are trapped in a toxic relationship or just stuck with the wrong person, making the decision to leave a relationship – especially a long term one – is never easy. We all need to be 100% sure we are doing the right thing before we take the final decision, so that we do not regret anything later. Hopefully, this book can help you in this situation when you are contemplating ending your relationship, but aren't sure of your reasons.

If you have already finished reading the book, you have noticed that it has been divided into three parts – each part to help you through a specific time of your process. I have described in detail everything that I thought would come in handy before, during and after your breakup or divorce. What you need to think about before taking the decision to break up, what to do while you are trying to break up, and what to do after the breakup

I have used my years of research and experience in writing this book. If I can help you just a little bit in making the right decision, I would consider myself successful and content. All the best!

About the author

Dr. Mary Ann Martínez is a Board Certified Clinical Mental Health Counselor. She specialized in Sex Therapy, and Marriage and Family Therapy. Her experience spans more than 25 years in clinical practice and 30 years in higher education.

Dr. Martínez is a Certified Mentor, Consultant, and a member of the Puerto Rico Examination Board of Professional Counselors. Is a producer and member of various panels on social media and radio and is also the host of the video-podcast _De Terapias y Terapeutas_ (About Therapies and Therapists). She is a speaker, lecturer, and author.

Dr. Mary Ann Martinez is also an Ordained Minister of the Church of God Movement (Church of God, Anderson IN).

Other books by the author

- Anger Management: Understanding anger and finding the right way to deal with it

- Completa Imperfección: Libérate de la seducción del perfeccionismo y disfruta tu vida

- Birth Control and Safe Sex: Sex secrets every couple needs to know

- Lea La Biblia en un Año: Guía Básica – 7 Planes de lectura para leer la Biblia

www.ingramcontent.com/pod-product-compliance
Lightning Source LLC
Chambersburg PA
CBHW060853280326
41934CB00007B/1024